GUN CONTROL

Opposing
Viewpoints®

Other Books of Related Interest

Opposing
Viewpoints®

GUN CONTROL

Helen Cothran, *Book Editor*

Daniel Leone, *President*
Bonnie Szumski, *Publisher*
Scott Barbour, *Managing Editor*

OPPOSING
VIEWPOINTS®
SERIES

GREENHAVEN
PRESS®

THOMSON
—————✳—————™
GALE

San Diego • Detroit • New York • San Francisco • Cleveland
New Haven, Conn. • Waterville, Maine • London • Munich

© 2003 by Greenhaven Press. Greenhaven Press is an imprint of The Gale Group, Inc.,
a division of Thomson Learning, Inc.

Greenhaven® and Thomson Learning™ are trademarks used herein under license.

For more information, contact
Greenhaven Press
27500 Drake Rd.
Farmington Hills, MI 48331-3535
Or you can visit our Internet site at http://www.gale.com

LIBRARY OF CONGRESS CATALOGING-IN-PUBLICATION DATA

Gun control : opposing viewpoints / Helen Cothran, book editor.
     p. cm. — (Opposing viewpoints series)
  Includes bibliographical references and index.
  ISBN 0-7377-0746-1 (pbk : alk. paper) — ISBN 0-7377-0747-X (hb : alk. paper)
     1. Gun control—United States. 2. Firearms ownership—United States.
  I. Cothran, Helen. II. Opposing viewpoints series (Unnumbered)
  HV7436 .G8677 2003
  363.3'3'0973—dc21   2002023622

Printed in the United States of America

"Congress shall make
no law...abridging the
freedom of speech, or of
the press."

First Amendment to the U.S. Constitution

The basic foundation of our democracy is the First
Amendment guarantee of freedom of expression.
The Opposing Viewpoints Series is dedicated to the
concept of this basic freedom and the idea that it is
more important to practice it than to enshrine it.

Contents

Why Consider Opposing Viewpoints?

"The only way in which a human being can make some approach to knowing the whole of a subject is by hearing what can be said about it by persons of every variety of opinion and studying all modes in which it can be looked at by every character of mind. No wise man ever acquired his wisdom in any mode but this."

John Stuart Mill

In our media-intensive culture it is not difficult to find differing opinions. Thousands of newspapers and magazines and dozens of radio and television talk shows resound with differing points of view. The difficulty lies in deciding which opinion to agree with and which "experts" seem the most credible. The more inundated we become with differing opinions and claims, the more essential it is to hone critical reading and thinking skills to evaluate these ideas. Opposing Viewpoints books address this problem directly by presenting stimulating debates that can be used to enhance and teach these skills. The varied opinions contained in each book examine many different aspects of a single issue. While examining these conveniently edited opposing views, readers can develop critical thinking skills such as the ability to compare and contrast authors' credibility, facts, argumentation styles, use of persuasive techniques, and other stylistic tools. In short, the Opposing Viewpoints Series is an ideal way to attain the higher-level thinking and reading skills so essential in a culture of diverse and contradictory opinions.

In addition to providing a tool for critical thinking, Opposing Viewpoints books challenge readers to question their own strongly held opinions and assumptions. Most people form their opinions on the basis of upbringing, peer pressure, and personal, cultural, or professional bias. By reading carefully balanced opposing views, readers must directly confront new ideas as well as the opinions of those with whom they disagree. This is not to simplistically argue that everyone who reads opposing views will—or should—change his or her opinion. Instead, the series enhances readers' understanding of their own views by encouraging confrontation with opposing ideas. Careful examination of others' views can lead to the readers' understanding of the logical inconsistencies in their own opinions, perspective on why they hold an opinion, and the consideration of the possibility that their opinion requires further evaluation.

Evaluating Other Opinions

To ensure that this type of examination occurs, Opposing Viewpoints books present all types of opinions. Prominent spokespeople on different sides of each issue as well as well-known professionals from many disciplines challenge the reader. An additional goal of the series is to provide a forum for other, less known, or even unpopular viewpoints. The opinion of an ordinary person who has had to make the decision to cut off life support from a terminally ill relative, for example, may be just as valuable and provide just as much insight as a medical ethicist's professional opinion. The editors have two additional purposes in including these less known views. One, the editors encourage readers to respect others' opinions—even when not enhanced by professional credibility. It is only by reading or listening to and objectively evaluating others' ideas that one can determine whether they are worthy of consideration. Two, the inclusion of such viewpoints encourages the important critical thinking skill of objectively evaluating an author's credentials and bias. This evaluation will illuminate an author's reasons for taking a particular stance on an issue and will aid in readers' evaluation of the author's ideas.

It is our hope that these books will give readers a deeper understanding of the issues debated and an appreciation of the complexity of even seemingly simple issues when good and honest people disagree. This awareness is particularly important in a democratic society such as ours in which people enter into public debate to determine the common good. Those with whom one disagrees should not be regarded as enemies but rather as people whose views deserve careful examination and may shed light on one's own.

Thomas Jefferson once said that "difference of opinion leads to inquiry, and inquiry to truth." Jefferson, a broadly educated man, argued that "if a nation expects to be ignorant and free . . . it expects what never was and never will be." As individuals and as a nation, it is imperative that we consider the opinions of others and examine them with skill and discernment. The Opposing Viewpoints Series is intended to help readers achieve this goal.

David L. Bender and Bruno Leone,
Founders

Greenhaven Press anthologies primarily consist of previously published material taken from a variety of sources, including periodicals, books, scholarly journals, newspapers, government documents, and position papers from private and public organizations. These original sources are often edited for length and to ensure their accessibility for a young adult audience. The anthology editors also change the original titles of these works in order to clearly present the main thesis of each viewpoint and to explicitly indicate the opinion presented in the viewpoint. These alterations are made in consideration of both the reading and comprehension levels of a young adult audience. Every effort is made to ensure that Greenhaven Press accurately reflects the original intent of the authors included in this anthology.

Introduction

*"What is left for the supporters of restrictive gun control
seeking an intellectual justification for their position?
They are counting on a complete rewrite of American
history [to downplay the centrality of guns in America]."*
—*Clayton E. Cramer,* author of Concealed Weapon
Laws of the Early Republic: Dueling, Southern
Violence, and Moral Reform

*"If America's gun culture is a recent development, then
gun deaths today . . . are not the price we pay for our
heritage—because there is no such heritage."*
—*Joshua Sugarmann, executive director
of the Violence Policy Center*

American actors such as John Wayne brought the cowboy—icon of American independence, righteousness, and
brawn—to the silver screen. Moviegoers around the world
have come to associate the United States with cowboys, and,
for better or ill, with the guns that they carry.

America's fascination with guns and the implications of
that attraction—such as over ten thousand murders committed with firearms in the United States in 1996—have come
under contentious debate in recent years. Gun proponents
such as David Kopel, research director of the Independence
Institute, a free-market think tank, contend that guns have
played a major role in the nation's history. On the contrary,
Michael A. Bellesiles, professor of history at Emory University, argues that America's historic gun culture is "an invented tradition." The debate surrounding the history of
guns in America has far-reaching implications. On the one
hand, gun advocates argue that if guns have always been central to American culture then we must continue to live with
them. In consequence, gun bans and other gun control measures run counter to American values. On the other hand,
gun control advocates assert that if guns have not been central to American culture then we need not live with them

and their dangers. These analysts conclude that gun control is not only acceptable but necessary.

Gun advocates such as Kopel argue that America's earliest experience with guns shaped its national character. Kopel contends that "for the few people who would be called 'Americans,' life itself would have been impossible without firearms" as protection against Indians and for hunting. These commentators argue that early Americans were at ease with guns. Some analysts maintain that only after modern gun control measures created a stigma against gun ownership did gun violence become a serious problem in the United States. Once guns became stigmatized, young people no longer grew up with firearms or learned to use them responsibly. Instead, they became tools for violent crime. Gun advocates assert that gun control is not only ineffective at reducing violent crime but is un-American as well.

However, some analysts disagree about the historic prevalence of guns in the United States. For example, Bellesiles contends that "gun ownership was exceptional in the seventeenth, eighteenth, and early nineteenth centuries, even on the frontier." He claims that America's gun culture grew with the gun industry during industrialization around the time of the Civil War. Gun manufacturers invented the idea that guns were central to America's identity, he argues, because such a cultural mystique helped sell their products. After the Civil War, with so many more firearms available, gun violence increased, according to Bellesiles. Many gun critics point to Bellesiles' work as evidence for the need for gun control. They reason that if gun violence rose after guns became more available, clearly guns lead to violence. Regulating access to guns, then, will reduce gun violence.

Due to pressure by gun critics, various gun control measures have been enacted over the last fifty years. For example, in 1968, the Gun Control Act, which banned gun sales to most criminals, was passed. In 1994 Congress passed an assault weapon ban. However, commentators continue to debate whether such measures are necessary or effective.

Those against gun control contend that laws restricting the use of guns endanger the lives of citizens because more guns are used for self-defense than are used to commit crime.

In consequence, easy availability of guns actually reduces violent crime rates. For instance, many analysts claim that states that allow citizens to carry concealed weapons experience lower violent crime rates than states that have restrictive concealed-carry laws. Many analysts also point to rising crime rates in other countries that have passed strict gun control measures as proof that gun control does not work.

In contrast, gun control advocates contend that firearms regulations are needed to take guns out of the hands of criminals. These commentators contend that violent crime rates rise when more individuals own guns. Gun violence creates countless injuries and deaths as well, they argue, the costs of which are borne by taxpayers. Many gun control proponents are especially concerned about the dangers of guns to children. They point to school shootings as evidence that guns are a serious risk to the nation's children.

Support for or opposition to gun control in some measure depends upon the public's understanding of American history. The cowboy—and for many, the gun that he carries—has come to symbolize the American spirit. Yet the notion that guns are central to Americans' identity has been increasingly challenged by those who favor stricter gun regulations. The authors in *Opposing Viewpoints: Gun Control* debate whether gun control is necessary and effective in the following chapters: Does Private Gun Ownership Pose a Serious Threat to Society? Does the Constitution Protect Private Gun Ownership? Is Gun Ownership an Effective Means of Self-Defense? What Measures Would Reduce Gun Violence? To be sure, any measures that are taken to regulate guns will certainly collide with America's gun history, which—real or fabricated—strongly governs attitudes about the role of firearms in American society.

CHAPTER 1

Does Private Gun Ownership Pose a Serious Threat to Society?

Chapter Preface

While newspapers and television newscasts frequently report on the dangers of privately owned guns, gun advocates accuse the media of exaggerating the extent of gun violence in order to gain support for gun control measures. For example, the *New York Times* reported in 2000 that the "incidence of . . . rampage killings appears to have increased [in the past decade]." However, economists John R. Lott Jr. and William Landes claim that those findings are untrue and assert that "the number [of rampage killings] is not changing much over time."

The Media Research Center—which documents what it claims to be bias in the media—reviewed gun control stories on several television broadcasts from July 1, 1995, through June 30, 1997. The analysts concluded that antigun stories outnumbered progun stories on the networks by a ratio of eleven to one. Moreover, a national media analysis done by Brian Patrick, a doctoral candidate at the University of Michigan, compared the coverage of the progun National Rifle Association (NRA) in prestigious newspapers. Patrick argues that there is "systematic marginalization of the NRA."

However, many prominent organizations claim that the media is merely reporting what is true—that widespread private gun ownership in the United States has resulted in extremely high rates of lethal violence. For example, the Violence Policy Center—which provides an array of statistics on gun violence in the United States—claims that "the United States leads the industrialized world in firearms violence of all types. . . . Most of this violence involves the use of a handgun." Many media commentators charge that gun lobbying groups such as the NRA distort the facts in order to minimize the extent of gun violence and further the interests of their members.

Charges of bias and distortion from analysts on both sides of the gun control issue make it difficult to assess what role privately owned guns play in lethal violence. In the following chapter, experts from both camps debate whether private gun ownership poses a serious threat to society.

"There is a gun crisis in the United States. Between 1933 and 1982, nearly one million Americans were killed by firearms."

Private Gun Ownership Leads to Higher Rates of Gun Violence

Violence Policy Center

The Violence Policy Center is an educational foundation that conducts research on firearms violence. In the following viewpoint, the center argues that an increase in private gun ownership has led to an explosion in the number of Americans killed by firearms in murders, suicides, and accidents. According to the center, most of those killed by firearms are murdered at the hands of a relation or acquaintance, not a criminal. The organization maintains that guns should be regulated like any other dangerous consumer product.

As you read, consider the following questions:
1. According to the 1989 Centers for Disease Control study cited by the authors, what was the economic cost of firearms violence in 1985?
2. How many times in 1992 were handguns used by law-abiding citizens to kill criminals justifiably, according to the Violence Policy Center?
3. According to the organization, what was the firearms suicide rate in 1975?

There is a gun crisis in the United States. Between 1933 and 1982, nearly one million Americans were killed by firearms in murders, suicides and accidents. Since 1960 alone, more than half a million have died as the result of gun injuries. In 1992, at least 35,000 died by gunfire. Today, among all consumer products, only cars outpace guns as a cause of fatal injury, and guns will likely pass them by 2003.

The Crisis

The explosion in the country's homicide and suicide rates has paralleled a corresponding boom in its firearms population. Usually purchased for self-defense, the easily concealable and portable handgun is used in the vast majority of gun violence—even though it is outnumbered two to one by such traditional long guns as sporting rifles and shotguns. The increased popularity of high-caliber, high-capacity semiautomatic handguns—both in standard and assault-weapon configurations—has added to the carnage. "Well, they have more holes in them now," a Washington trauma surgeon replied when asked to describe the changes he'd seen in gunshot victims over the past decade. "And the holes are a lot bigger."

In addition to those killed, firearms account for an untabulated number of injuries. In 1972, the National Health Interview Survey estimated that the ratio of nonfatal shootings to fatal was five to one. Using this figure, in 1988 (the most recent year for which complete figures are available), nearly 153,000 Americans were injured by firearms.

In addition to the human toll, the monetary cost—as measured in hospitalization, rehabilitation and lost wages—is staggering. A 1989 Centers for Disease Control study estimated the lifetime economic cost of firearms violence for 1985 at $14.4 billion, ranking it third in economic toll for all injury categories.

During the same period that firearms violence escalated, the organized gun control movement established itself as a permanent player. Unlike others involved in public-policy debates, however, gun-control advocates have tended to work from an extremely limited base of knowledge, steadfast in their refusal to undertake the research necessary to design a truly comprehensive plan to curtail firearms violence.

Legislation to halt gun violence has often been developed on an ad hoc, piecemeal basis to meet specific threats posed by the firearms industry or to cater to the public's sympathies. And while other movements have relied on the plight of victims to draw attention to their research and policy proposals, the gun control movement has little to offer beyond a "victim's strategy."

In order to avoid the tragedy of passing laws that prove unworkable or ineffective, gun-control advocates must be willing to jettison out-of-date concepts and solutions. It is the basic premise of this study that the first step in expanding the conceptual framework of the debate is to recognize firearms for what they are: inherently dangerous consumer products. Only from this recognition can a comprehensive regulatory approach to firearms—similar to those that exist for virtually all other dangerous consumer products—be created.

The Issue Isn't Crime

Faced with the staggering facts of crime and living under a barrage of TV and movie images that reinforce the link between crime and guns, Americans unsurprisingly equate firearms misuse with criminal violence. The phrase *gun violence* conjures a host of stereotypical images: robbers lurking in dark alleys; street gangs; convenience-store holdups. Recent additions include crazed loners rampaging through fast-food restaurants and embittered ex-employees returning to former work sites to seek retribution.

Contrary to popular perception, however, most murders do not occur as the result of an attack by a stranger but stem from an argument between people who know each other and often are related. For murders in 1992, for example, in which the relationship and circumstances were reported (61 percent of all murders):

- Almost half of the victims were either related to (12 percent) or acquainted with (35 percent) their killers. Only 14 percent were killed by strangers. Twenty-nine percent of female victims were slain by their husbands or boyfriends.
- Twenty-nine percent stemmed from arguments, com-

pared with 23 percent resulting from actual or suspected felonious activity.

- Ninety-four percent of black murder victims were slain by black offenders. Eighty-three percent of white victims were killed by white offenders. In addition to being intraracial, murder is also intragender for men. In single victim/single slayer situations, 87 percent of all male victims were slain by a male offender. Nine out of 10 female victims, however, were slain by a male.

The crazed loner and the robber in the alley do exist. What FBI statistics reveal and police officers have long known is that most homicide does not result from criminal attacks or pre-meditated murders. The majority of firearms homicide stems from arguments that turn deadly because of ready access to a gun. As the country's firearms population has increased, so has its per capita homicide rate. From 1963 to 1973, the per capita homicide rate more than doubled: from 4.3 per 100,000 to 9.3 per 100,000. During this same period, the nation's handgun population tripled.

A more striking contrast comes from comparing firearms with nonfirearms homicide trends for the same period. The nonfirearms homicide rate increased 55 percent, from 2 per 100,000 in 1963 to 3.1 per 100,000 in 1973. The firearms homicide rate, however, jumped 148 percent, from 2.5 per 100,000 in 1963 to 6.2 per 100,000 in 1973.

The Issue Isn't Self Defense

Without doubt, handguns and other firearms stop crimes and kill criminals. The question is, how often? Anecdotal evidence is offered each month in the Armed Citizen, a column in the National Rifle Association's (NRA) *American Rifleman* magazine. The column offers an assortment of self-defense gun incidents culled from newspapers across the country, and each one begins with the same statement: "Studies indicate that firearms are used over one million times a year for personal protection and the presence of a firearm, without a shot being fired, prevents crime in many instances." That claim comes from NRA polls and from research conducted by Gary Kleck, a professor of criminology at Florida State University. But the flaws in Kleck's research are evident to even the most casual reader; among those who have questioned his analysis and methodology is the National Research Council of the National Academy of Sciences.

Those who argue that handguns are in truth rarely used to kill criminals or stop crimes point to information tabulated by the FBI and the Bureau of Justice Statistics. The FBI's *Uniform Crime Reports* defines a justifiable homicide as "the killing of a felon by a law-enforcement officer in the line of duty, or the killing of a felon during the commission of a felony by a private citizen." In 1992, handguns were used only 262 times by law-abiding citizens to kill criminals justifiably.

Addicted to Gun Violence

Gun violence in America is as common as the sunrise. And even as we express our collective horror at [school shooting tragedies], the truth is that we are addicted to gun violence. We celebrate it, romanticize it, eroticize it. Above all, we market it—through movies, videos, television, radio, books, magazines and newspapers.

Bob Herbert, *New York Times*, January 1, 2001.

Although the *Uniform Crime Reports* offers no information on nonlethal self-defense firearms use, the Bureau of Justice Statistics' National Crime Victimization Survey does. What is most striking is how rarely firearms are used in self-defense. In 1987, in only one-half of one percent of all intended or actual incidences of violent crime was a firearm available to the potential or actual victim—both gun owning and non–gun owning. For that year the National Crime Victimization Survey estimates that there were 5,660,570 violent crimes (attempted and completed) in the United States. Using these figures, there were approximately 28,000 instances in which there was a firearm available to the victim. And of these instances it's not even known whether the gun was used successfully to stop the crime.

These figures pale in comparison with the tens of thousands who die from firearms each year and the more than 150,000 injured annually. Research has consistently shown that a gun in the home is far more likely to be used in suicide, murder or fatal accidents than to kill a criminal. A 1988 study of gun deaths in King County, Wash., for the period from 1978 to 1983, conducted by Dr. Arthur Kellermann, found that for every time a firearm was used in a self-protection homicide, 37 lives were lost in gun suicides, 4.6 lives were lost in gun homicides, and 1.3 lives were lost via unintentional gun deaths—43 deaths for every self-defense homicide. A second Kellermann study, released in October 1993, showed that keeping a gun in the home increased the risk of homicide nearly threefold.

On the national level, using FBI figures, for every time a citizen used a handgun in 1992 in a justifiable homicide, 48 lives were ended in handgun murders. By including the estimated 12,500 handgun suicides that occurred that year, the ratio of lives lost for every justifiable homicide jumps to 95 to one.

The Ignored Gun Deaths: Suicides

For all the fear and fascination with guns and murder, the fact remains that most gun deaths are not a result of murder but suicide. But if crime has become inextricably linked with the gun debate, suicide has remained strangely ignored. Because it doesn't fit easily into either pro- or anti-gun control schematics, it has been treated as something of an embarrassment.

Those with pro-gun sympathies tend to brush the subject aside with the assertion that suicide victims would find a way to kill themselves "no matter what." To the pro-control side, a focus on suicide contradicts the perception that firearms violence results from guns finding their way into criminal hands. Any effort to address suicide requires the abandonment of the gun-control-as-crime-control argument and the acknowledgement that the problem lies with guns not only in criminal hands but also in the hands of the law-abiding.

As with murder, the increase in the suicide rate has paralleled the increase in the country's firearms population. In 1962 the overall suicide rate stood at 10.9 per 100,000, with a firearms suicide rate of 5.1 per 100,000 (accounting for 46.8 percent of the 20,203 reported suicides that year). By 1975 the overall suicide rate reached 12.7 per 100,000, while the firearms suicide rate hit seven per 100,000.

Like murders, most gun suicides are not committed with weapons purchased specifically for the attempt but with those already available. It is estimated that only about 10 percent of suicides by firearm are committed with firearms purchased specifically for the suicide. As a result, the usual gun-control schemes—background checks, licensing, registration, safety training—would have little effect.

With the increased marketing of firearms—specifically handguns—to women for self-defense, patterns of female suicide have also changed. In 1970 poisoning was the suicide method most commonly used by women. This means has decreased in inverse proportion to gun use. Now, like men, women most often kill themselves with firearms. . . .

A Logical Approach to Gun Violence

Honored by some as icons of freedom or modern-day talismans to ward off crime, denigrated by others as forces of evil in and of themselves, handguns are difficult for many Americans to consider as simply another consumer product. To think of guns as some form of dangerous toaster is to disparage them. Yet if we strip away the mythology and apply the same standards that we would apply to toasters—or lawn darts, DDT or baby cribs—a far more logical and effective approach to gun violence begins to take shape.

> "*Handgun ownership has increased about
> 3.5 times more than the population
> increase since the end of World War
> II—with no comparable increase in the
> murder rate.*"

Private Gun Ownership Does Not Lead to Higher Rates of Gun Violence

Don B. Kates Jr.

Don B. Kates Jr. is a criminological policy analyst with the Pacific Research Institute in San Francisco and coauthor, with Gary Kleck, of *The Great American Gun War: Essays in Firearms and Violence*. Kates contends in the following viewpoint that an increase in private gun ownership over the last fifty years has not resulted in higher rates of gun violence. He concedes that there have been brief periods when gun buying and murder rates did increase together, but he contends that gun buying did not *cause* the increase in murders. On the contrary, Kates asserts that it is more likely that more people bought guns to defend themselves in response to increasing murder rates.

As you read, consider the following questions:
1. According to Kates, during what period did American homicide rates and the number of firearms owned both rapidly increase?
2. In Kates's opinion, why do people buy guns?
3. How do gun control advocates support their claim that increased gun ownership causes an increase in homicide rates, according to the author?

A nti-gun advocates present their position as pragmatic and intellectually based, specifically as a program for eliminating the widespread ownership of firearms, a phenomenon they believe to be a (or the) major cause of murder in America. Despite this facade of rationalism, what the anti-gun position actually rests on is intellectual confusion, abetted, it must be said, by a credulous desire to believe. That desire alone explains how believers in the anti-gun faith credulously accept concepts they would instantly reject as absurd in any other context.

Logical Fallacies

Consider the fallacious argument from correlation that so many otherwise intelligent and skeptical people credulously swallowed 30 years ago—and have since never reexamined. For a brief period in the 1960s and early 1970s, the American homicide rate and the number of firearms owned were both rapidly increasing at the same time. The argument seriously advanced then, and consistently maintained ever since by many anti-gun advocates, is that a correlation of more guns and more homicide proves that the widespread availability of guns is a primary cause of murder.

This is a simple-minded confusion of cause and effect. In the late 1970s, California State University economist Joseph Magaddino compared it to a basketball team, noting the correlation that the temperature in the auditorium goes up when their games attract large numbers of spectators—and concluding that the way to attract more fans is to turn the heat up in the auditorium.

The fact is that a mere correlation between increases in gun buying and in homicide does not and cannot prove guns cause murder. Assuming that there is any cause and effect relationship, the most obvious one is the reverse, i.e., that it was the rise in murders that caused increased gun buying. Alternatively, the upsurges in both murders and gun sales may have been caused by a third factor, e.g., the enormous increase in burglary and violent crime that also began in the 1960s.

Taken either together or separately, these crime-causes-guns explanations are far more plausible than the guns-cause-murder explanation [prompted by] the brief 1960–70s correlation between increases in gun buying and in murder. It is virtually self-evident that people buy guns in response to dramatically increasing crime in general and murders in particular. Indeed, so clearly true is it that fear drives gun ownership that anti-gun advocates themselves agree—adding, however, that people's natural urge to protect their families should be prohibited because gun ownership is "the principal cause of murder."

The Relative Risks of Gun Violence

In 1997, whereas homicides with a gun took 15,551 lives and 1,500 died from firearms accidents, 88,000 died from pneumonia and flu, 91,000 from accidents (I've subtracted the 1,500 firearms accidents), 110,000 from lung diseases, 159,000 from strokes, 537,000 from cancer and 725,000 from heart disease.

Charley Reese, (San Diego) *North County Times*, June 23, 1999.

Note that this guns-cause-murder notion is a bare speculation that is not supported by the brief 1960s–70s correlation of more guns and more murder. That correlation fails to support the guns-cause-murder speculation because that correlation is independently explained by the accepted fact that people react to crime and violence by acquiring guns. Neither in the 1960s nor today is there intellectual support for the claim that guns are the "primary" cause of murder. The belief that there is such support is a mere intellectual confusion based on credulous desire to believe.

Credulity and Ignorance

Only that credulity, and/or sheer ignorance, explains how the anti-gun view continues today when decades of post-1960s evidence have reduced the anti-gun view from an unsupported speculation to a clearly erroneous one. This evidence arises from an unarguable point: If guns really were a (or the) primary cause of murder, an enormous increase in guns would necessarily lead to a more or less comparably large increase in the murder rate. The fact is that handgun ownership has increased about 3.5 times more than the population increase since the end of World War II—with no comparable increase in the murder rate.

Space does not permit detailed review of the statistics. Readers who are interested should consult the May 2000 issue of *Homicide Studies*, a criminology journal which carries an article I co-authored with Prof. Daniel Polsby. Our article's findings include such facts as that the homicide rate decreased 27.7 percent over the 25-year period 1973–97 despite increases of 160 percent in the number of civilian handguns and of 103 percent in guns of all kinds. (These increases far outstripped the population increase over that period.)

It is important to emphasize the limitations on our findings. They should not be confused with the conclusion of Yale Law School economist John Lott that increasing firearms availability actually decreases violent crime, based on statistics from before and after 30 states enacted laws under which concealed carry licenses are issued to every qualified applicant, and comparisons to the states that have not enacted such laws. While we do not disagree with Prof. Lott, his is a study of a specific law and is based on much more extensive data and a much more sophisticated methodology than ours. All our study does is discredit the theory that widespread gun ownership is a major cause of homicide. If that theory were valid, the enormous increases in guns over the post World War II period should have been—but were not—highly correlated with comparable homicide rate increases. Even more significant is that vast gun increases over the 25 most recent years coincided with a dramatic decrease in murder rates.

Evasion and Fraud

It bears emphasis that the anti-gun movement's failure to deal with such data involves not just intellectual confusion but evasion and fraud. Please understand that our article is not some feat of arduous research into arcane data. Any competent scholar could have duplicated our data in less than a week; indeed, any intelligent layperson with access to a university library could have done so. Moreover, anti-gun groups like Handgun Control, Inc. (HCI) would not have needed our article to know the general pattern: Over the

27

past 25 years the homicide rate exhibited only minor fluctuation, followed by substantial decline, despite a vast increase in the number of guns. Though our precise statistics would not be known, this general pattern is something anyone seriously interested in the relationship between guns and homicide would know.

If there were some way to reconcile that general pattern with the claim that widespread gun ownership is the primary cause of murder, surely someone would have announced it. Tellingly, since the mid-1970s anti-gun advocates have instead "supported" that claim with meaningless short-term homicide statistics. Remember that homicide rates are not static. It is easy for HCI, et al to say, as they regularly have, things like "In 1978 and 1979, over 8 million more guns were added to the existing stock and homicide increased by X percent." Saying that is also meaningless. It is a mere fluctuation, since in 1976 and 1977, homicide decreased by a comparable amount despite the fact that over 8 million more guns were added to the existing stock in those years.

To even begin to show by correlation that guns are the (or even a) major cause of American homicide would require showing a long-term, consistent correlation: Twenty or 30 years in which vast increases in guns were paralleled by vast increases in the murder rate. The lack of any such consistent pattern dooms the notion that guns are a major cause of homicide. (The fact that the actual pattern is the reverse suggests the opposite conclusion which Prof. Lott impressively supports with the data in his book *More Guns, Less Crime*.)

"Uncontrolled ownership and use of firearms, especially handguns, is a serious threat to the public's health."

Private Gun Ownership Is a Public-Health Hazard

Richard F. Corlin

Richard F. Corlin is president of the American Medical Association (AMA). In the following viewpoint, which was excerpted from a speech delivered at the annual meeting of the American Medical Association on June 20, 2001, Corlin argues that increasing rates of gun violence in the United States have become a serious health crisis. He contends that gun violence constitutes an epidemic because it kills thousands of Americans each year and spreads like a disease. He urges the American Medical Association to respond to this epidemic in the same manner that it approaches other serious diseases—with sound research, education, and cooperation with other health and government agencies.

As you read, consider the following questions:
1. According to Corlin, how many Americans died by gunfire in 1998?
2. How many children does gunfire kill per day in the United States, according to the author?
3. According to Corlin, how much money is spent on gun violence research for every year of life lost to gunfire?

Excerpted from "The Secrets of Gun Violence in America," by Richard F. Corlin, *Vital Speeches of the Day*, August 1, 2001. Copyright © 2001 by *Vital Speeches of the Day*. Reprinted with permission.

Thank you for joining me [this evening on June 20, 2001]. It's my great pleasure to introduce to you the friends, colleagues and family members, without whom, I would not have made it here tonight. And without whose presence, this wouldn't be a special evening for me.

The Way It Used to Be

I grew up in East Orange, New Jersey, in the 1940's and 1950's. My high school was a mosaic of racial and ethnic diversity—equal numbers of blacks and whites, some Puerto Ricans, and a few Asians. We'd fight among ourselves from time to time—sometimes between kids of the same race, sometimes equal opportunity battles between kids of different races and nationalities. Our fights were basically all the same: some yelling and shouting, then some shoving, a couple of punches, and then some amateur wrestling. They weren't gang fights—everyone but the two combatants just stood around and watched—until one of our teachers came over and broke it up.

My old high school reminds me a little of [the movie] "West Side Story" only without the switchblades or a Leonard Bernstein score. And there were no Sharks or Jets. Remember, those were the days of James Dean and Elvis Presley. Nobody pulled out a gun—none of us had them and no one even thought of having one. The worst wound anyone had after one of those fights was a split lip or a black eye.

It was just like kids have always been—until today. Back then, no parents in that town of mostly lower-middle class blue collar workers had to worry that their children might get shot at school, in the park or on the front stoop at home. But then again, that was also a time when we thought of a Columbine as a desert flower, not a high school in Littleton, Colorado [where in April 1999, twelve students and a teacher were shot and killed by two male high school students].

Even in my first encounter with medicine, when I was only 14 years old and got a summer job at Presbyterian Hospital in Newark, New Jersey, there were no guns. I worked on what was called the utility team—moving patients back to their own rooms after surgery, starting IVs, taking EKGs and passing N-G tubes [nasogastric tubes used for feeding patients]. I told them I wanted to be a doctor and—unbelievably at the age of 14—they let me help the pathologist perform autopsies. I was so excited about helping with the autopsies that I used to repeat the details to my mom and dad over dinner. Before long, they made me eat by myself in the kitchen.

When I was old enough to get a driver's license, I got a job working as an emergency room aide and ambulance driver at Elizabeth General Hospital. In all that time, in five summers of working in two center city hospitals—in the recovery room, in the morgue, in the emergency room, and driving the ambulance—I never saw even one gunshot victim.

The Ubiquity of Guns

Today, it's very different. Guns are so available and violence so commonplace that some doctors now see gunshot wounds every week—if not every day. It's as if guns have replaced fists as the playground weapon of choice. The kids certainly think so. In a nationwide poll taken in March after two students were shot to death at Santana High School near San Diego, almost half of the 500 high school students surveyed said it wouldn't be difficult for them to get a gun. And one in five high school boys said they had carried a weapon to school in the last 12 months. One in five. Frightening, isn't it?

I began by telling you how I grew up in a world without guns. That has changed for me—as it has for so many Americans. Recently, the violence of guns touched me personally. Not long ago, Trish, one of our office staff members in my practice—a vibrant, hard-working young woman from Belize—was gunned down while leaving a holiday party at her aunt's home in Los Angeles.

Trish had done nothing wrong—some might say that she was in the wrong place at the wrong time—but I don't buy into that. Here was a woman who was where she should be—leaving a relative's home—when she was gunned down. Someone drove down the street randomly firing an assault weapon out the car window, and he put a bullet through her eye. Trish lingered in a coma for eight days—and then she died, an innocent victim of gun violence.

With the preponderance of weapons these days, it comes as no surprise that gun violence—both self-inflicted and against others—is now a serious public health crisis. No one can avoid its brutal and ugly presence. No one. Not physicians. Not the public. And most certainly—not the politicians—no matter how much they might want to.

Let me tell you about part of the problem. In the 1990s, the Centers for Disease Control and Prevention (CDC) had a system in place for collecting data about the results of gun violence. But Congress took away its funding, thanks to heavy lobbying by the anti–gun control groups. You see, the gun lobby doesn't want gun violence addressed as a public health issue. Because that data would define the very public health crisis that these powerful interests don't want acknowledged. And they fear that such evidence-based data could be used to gain support to stop the violence. Which, of course, means talking about guns and the deaths and injuries associated with them.

The Costs of Gun Violence

The estimated medical costs of treating the gunshot injuries received during 1994 in the United States was $2.3 billion. The average medical cost of a gunshot injury was approximately $17,000, of which 49% was borne by taxpayers, 18% by private insurance, and 33% by other sources. While medical costs are a relatively small component of the total burden imposed on society by gun violence, they represent a substantial cost to the medical care system.

Philip J. Cook et al., *JAMA*, August 4, 1999.

We all know that violence of every kind is a pervasive threat to our society. And the greatest risk factor associated with that violence—is access to firearms. Because—there's no doubt about it—guns make the violence more violent and deadlier.

Now my speech today is not a polemic. It is not an attack on the politics or the profits or the personalities associated with guns in our society. It isn't even about gun control. I want to talk to you about the public health crisis itself—and how we can work to address it; in the same way we have worked to address other public health crises such as polio, tobacco, and drunk driving.

At the American Medical Association (AMA), we acknowledged the epidemic of gun violence when—in 1987—our House of Delegates first set policy on firearms. The House recognized the irrefutable truth that "uncontrolled ownership and use of firearms, especially handguns, is a serious threat to the public's health inasmuch as the weapons are one of the main causes of intentional and unintentional injuries and death." In 1993 and 1994, we resolved that the AMA would, among other actions, "support scientific research and objective discussion aimed at identifying causes of and solutions to the crime and violence problem."

The Science

Scientific research and objective discussion because we as physicians are—first and foremost—scientists. We need to look at the science of the subject, the data, and—if you will—the micro-data, before we make a diagnosis. Not until then can we agree upon the prognosis or decide upon a course of treatment.

First, let's go straight to the science that we do know. How does this disease present itself? Since 1962, more than a million Americans have died in firearm suicides, homicides and unintentional injuries. In 1998 alone, 30,708 Americans died by gunfire:

- 17,424 in firearm suicides
- 12,102 in firearm homicides
- 866 in unintentional shootings

Also in 1998, more than 64,000 people were treated in emergency rooms for non-fatal firearm injuries.

This is a uniquely American epidemic. In the same year that more than 30,000 people were killed by guns in America, the number in Germany was 1,164, in Canada, it was 1,034, in Australia 391, in England and Wales 211, and in Japan, the number for the entire year was 83.

The Delivery System

Next, let's look at how the disease spreads, what is its vector, or delivery system. To do that, we need to look at the gun market today. Where the hard, cold reality is—guns are more deadly than ever. Gun manufacturers—in the pursuit of technological innovation and profit—have steadily increased the lethality of firearms. The gun industry's need for new products and new models to stimulate markets that are already oversupplied with guns—has driven their push to innovate. Newer firearms mean more profits. With the American gun manufacturers producing more than 4.2 million new guns per year—and imports adding another 2.2 million annually—you'd think the market would be saturated.

But that's why they have to sell gun owners new guns for their collections—because guns rarely wear out. Hardly anyone here is driving their grandfather's 1952 Plymouth. But a lot of people probably have their grandfather's 1952 revolver. So gun manufacturers make guns that hold more rounds of ammunition, increase the power of that ammunition, and make guns smaller and easier to conceal.

These changes make guns better suited for crime, because they are easy to carry and more likely to kill or maim whether they are used intentionally or unintentionally. In fact, one of the most popular handgun types today is the so-called "pocket rocket": a palm-sized gun that is easy to conceal, has a large capacity for ammunition and comes in a high caliber.

The *Chicago Tribune* reported that the number of pocket rockets found at crime scenes nationwide almost tripled from 1995 to 1997. It was a pocket rocket in the hands of a self-proclaimed white supremacist that shot 5 children at the North Valley Jewish Community Center and killed a Filipino-American postal worker outside of Los Angeles in August of 1999.

Consumer Safety

Now, we don't regulate guns in America. We do regulate other dangerous products like cars and prescription drugs and tobacco and alcohol—but not guns. Gun sales information is not public. Gun manufacturers are exempt by federal law from the standard health and safety regulations that are applied to all other consumer products manufactured and sold in the United States.

No federal agency is allowed to exercise oversight over the gun industry to ensure consumer safety. In fact, no other consumer industry in the United States—not even the tobacco industry—has been allowed to so totally evade accountability for the harm their products cause to human beings. Just the gun industry.

In a similar pattern to the marketing of tobacco—which kills its best customers in the United States at a rate of 430,000 per year—the spread of gun-related injuries and death is especially tragic when it involves our children. Like young lungs and tar and nicotine—young minds are especially responsive to the deadliness of gun violence. . . .

What Should Be Done

We need to teach our children from the beginning that violence does have consequences—serious consequences—all the time. Gunfire kills 10 children a day in America. In fact, the United States leads the world in the rate at which its children die from firearms. The CDC recently analyzed firearm-related deaths in 26 countries for children under the age of 15—and found that 86 percent of all those deaths—occurred in the United States.

If this was a virus—or a defective car seat or an undercooked hamburger—killing our children, there would be a massive uproar within a week. Instead, our capacity to feel a sense of national shame has been diminished by the pervasiveness and numbing effect of all this violence.

We all are well aware of the extent of this threat to the nation's health. So why doesn't someone do something about it? . . .

Our mission [at the AMA] is not to abolish all guns from the hands of our fellow citizens. We're not advocating any limitations on hunting or the legitimate use of long guns, or for that matter, any other specific item of gun control. And we won't even be keeping a scorecard of legislative victories against guns in Congress and in the statehouses.

Why not? Because all these well-intentioned efforts have been tried by good people—and they have not met with success. Instead, they have been met with a well-organized, aggressive protest against their efforts by powerful lobbies in Washington and at the state and community levels. We—the American Medical Association—are going to take a different route—not just calls for advocacy—but for diplomacy and for statesmanship and for research as well. And make no mistake about this: We will not be co-opted by either the rhetoric or the agendas of the public policy "left" or "right" in this national debate about the safety and health of our citizens.

One of the ways we will do this is—to help assemble the data. Current, consistent, credible data are at the heart of epidemiology. What we don't know about violence—and guns—is literally killing us. And yet, very little is spent on researching gun-related injuries and deaths.

A recent study shows that for every year of life lost to heart disease, we spend $441 on research. For every year of life lost to cancer, we spend $794 on research. Yet for every year of life lost to gun violence, we spend only $31 on research. . . .

That's bad public policy. It's bad fiscal policy. And it certainly is bad medical policy. If we are to fight this epidemic of violence, the Centers for Disease Control [and Prevention] must have the budget and the authority to gather the data we need. As I mentioned earlier, the CDC's National Center for Injury Prevention and Control (NCIPC) researched the causes and prevention of many kinds of injuries. But in the mid-90's the gun lobby targeted the NCIPC—and scored a bull's eye when Congress eliminated its funding. It wasn't a lot of money—just $2.6 million—budget dust to the Federal government. But it meant the difference between existence and extinction for that project.

Just think—gun injuries cost our nation $2.3 billion in medical costs each year—yet some people think $2.6 million is too much to spend on tracking them. Every dollar spent on this research has the potential to reduce medical costs by $885. . . .

People have told me that [pursuing research on the gun violence epidemic] is a dangerous path to follow. That I am crazy to do it. That I am putting our organization in jeopardy. They say we'll lose members. They say we'll be the target of smear campaigns. They say that the most extremist of the gun supporters will seek to destroy us. But I believe that this is a battle we cannot not take on.

While there are indeed risks—the far greater risk for the health of the public, for us in this room, and for the AMA, is to do nothing. We, as physicians, and as the American Medical Association, have an ethical and moral responsibility to do this—as our mission statement says—"to promote the science and art of medicine and the betterment of public health." If removing the scourge of gun violence isn't bettering the public health—what is?

> "The medical literature [on gun violence is] biased, riddled with serious errors in facts, logic, and methodology, and thus utterly unreliable."

Private Gun Ownership Is Not a Public-Health Hazard

Miguel A. Faria Jr.

Miguel A. Faria Jr. is editor-in-chief of the *Medical Sentinel*, which is published by the Association of American Physicians and Surgeons. Faria contends in the following viewpoint that private gun ownership is not the public-health hazard that many in the medical community present it as. On the contrary, he claims that private gun ownership makes law-abiding citizens safer. Faria maintains that doctors and medical organizations conduct unreliable studies documenting the dangers of gun ownership because they are encouraged to do so by the gun-control lobby and often obtain federal money for undertaking such research.

As you read, consider the following questions:

1. According to Faria, what important fact about Seattle was ignored in John H. Sloan's study comparing that city's crime rates with Vancouver's?
2. How many lives are saved by guns for every life lost to them, according to Gary Kleck?
3. According to Faria, what percentage of all violent crimes are committed by hardened criminals and repeat offenders?

Excerpted from "The Tainted Public-Health Model of Gun Control," by Miguel A. Faria Jr., *Ideas on Liberty*, April 2001. Copyright © 2001 by Ideas on Liberty. Reprinted with permission.

E arly in the 1990s the American Medical Association (AMA) launched a major campaign against domestic violence, which continues to this day. As a concerned physician, neurosurgeon, and then an active member of organized medicine, I joined in what I considered a worthwhile cause.

Junk Science

It was then that I arrived at the unfortunate but inescapable conclusion that the integrity of science and medicine had been violated—and the public interest was not being served by the entrenched medical/public-health establishment—because of political expediency. To my consternation and great disappointment, when it came to the portrayal of firearms and violence, and the gun control "research" promulgated by public-health officials, it was obvious that the medical literature was biased, riddled with serious errors in facts, logic, and methodology, and thus utterly unreliable. Moreover, it had failed to objectively address both sides of this momentous issue, on which important public policy was being debated and formulated. And this was taking place despite the purported safeguards of peer review in the medical journals, the alleged claims of objectivity by medical editors, and the claims of impartiality by government-funded gun researchers in public health, particularly at the Centers for Disease Control and Prevention (CDC).

Over the next five years, particularly as editor of the *Journal of the Medical Association of Georgia*, I found that on the issue of violence, medical journals skirted sound scholarship and took the easy way out of the melee, presenting only one side of the story and suppressing the other. Those with dissenting views or research were excluded. The establishment was bent on presenting guns as a social ill and promoting draconian gun control at any price.

The most prestigious medical journal, the *New England Journal of Medicine* (NEJM), which claims openness to contrary views, is not immune to bias in this area. In fact, it is one of the most anti-gun publications in medical journalism. The NEJM routinely excludes articles that dissent from its well-known, strident, and inflexible position of gun-control advocacy. Editors have come and gone, but the governing board has made sure that the anti-gun position remains unaltered.

In "Bad Medicine—Doctors and Guns," Don B. Kates and associates describe a particularly egregious example of editorial bias by the NEJM. In 1988, two studies were independently submitted for publication. Both authors were affiliated with the University of Washington School of Public Health. One study, by Dr. John H. Sloan and others, was a *selective* two-city comparison of homicide rates between Vancouver, British Columbia, and Seattle, Washington. The other paper was a *comprehensive* comparison study between the United States and Canada by Dr. Brandon Centerwall.

Predictably, the editors chose to publish Sloan's article with inferior but favorable data claiming erroneously that severe gun-control policies had reduced Canadian homicides. They rejected Centerwall's superior study showing that such policies had not lowered the rate of homicides in Canada: the Vancouver homicide rate increased 25 percent after implementation of a 1977 Canadian law. Moreover, Sloan and associates glossed over the disparate ethnic compositions of Seattle and Vancouver. When the rates of homicides for whites are compared, in both of these cities, it turns out that the rate of homicide in Seattle is actually lower than in Vancouver. The important fact that blacks and Hispanics, who constitute higher proportions of the population in Seattle, have higher rates of homicides in that city was not mentioned.

Centerwall's paper on the comparative rates of homicides in the United States and Canada was finally published in the *American Journal of Epidemiology*, but his valuable research, unlike that of Sloan and his group, was not made widely available to the public. In contradistinction to his valuable gun-research data, Centerwall's other research pointing to the effects of TV violence on homicide rates has been made widely available; his data exculpating gun availability from high homicide rates in this country remains a closely guarded secret.

Over the years, the entrenched medical/public-health establishment, acting as a willing accomplice of the gun-control lobby has conducted politicized, results-oriented gun (control) research based on what can only be characterized as junk science. This has taken place not only because of ideology and political expediency, but also because of greed—federal money. Public health in general and gun control in particular were important areas where money was allocated by the Clinton administration, along with its repeated attempts at the federalization of the police force, erosion of civil liberties, and the implementation of a national identity card, all centerpieces of former President Bill Clinton's failed domestic crime-control policy.

But how was an agency like the CDC able to get in the gun-control business? Simply by propounding the erroneous notion that gun violence is a public-health issue and that crime is a disease, an epidemic—rather than a major facet of criminology. The public so deluded and the bureaucrats consequently empowered, public-health and CDC officials arrogated to themselves this new area of alleged expertise and espoused the preposterous but politically lucrative concept of guns and bullets as animated, virulent pathogens needing to be stamped out by limiting gun availability and ultimately confiscating guns from law-abiding citizens. Hard to believe in a constitutional republic with a Bill of Rights and a Second Amendment! Let me cite the following statement by CDC official Dr. Patrick O'Carroll as quoted in the *Journal of the American Medical Association* (JAMA, February 3, 1989): "Bringing about gun control, which itself covers a variety of activities from registration to confiscation was not the specific reason for the [CDC] section's creation. However, the facts themselves tend to make some form of regulation seem desirable. The way we're going to do this is to systematically build a case that owning firearms causes death."

Public-health officials and researchers conveniently neglect the fact that guns and bullets are inanimate objects that do not follow Koch's Postulates of Pathogenicity (a time-proven, simple, but logical series of scientific steps carried out by medical investigators to definitively prove a microorganism is pathogenic and directly responsible for causing a particular disease); and they fail to recognize the importance of individual responsibility and moral conduct—namely, that behind every shooting there is a person pulling the trigger who should be held accountable.

This portrayal of guns by the public-health establishment parallels the sensationalized reporting of violence and so-called "human interest" stories in the mainstream media; it exploits citizens' understandable concern about domestic violence and rampant street crime, but does not reflect the accurate, unbiased, and objective information that is needed for the formulation of sound public policy. In most instances, the public-health and medical establishments have become mouthpieces for the government's gun-control policies.

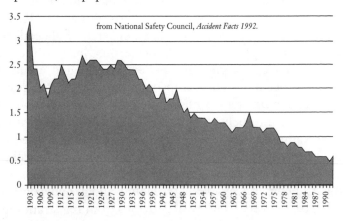

20th-Century U.S. Firearm Accident Rates
per 100,000 population

from National Safety Council, *Accident Facts 1992.*

Edgar A. Suter, *Journal of the Medical Association of Georgia*, March 1994.

As an example of biased research on which the CDC has squandered taxpayers' money is the work of prominent gun-control researcher Dr. Arthur Kellermann of Emory University's School of Public Health. Since at least the mid-1980s, Kellermann (and associates), whose work has been heavily funded by the CDC, has published a series of studies purporting to show that persons who keep guns in the home are more likely to be victims of homicide than those who don't. Despite the "peer reviewed" imprimatur of his published research, his studies, fraught with errors of facts, logic, and methodology, are published in the NEJM and JAMA with great fanfare (advance notices and press releases, followed by interviews and press conferences)—to the delight of the like-minded, cheerleading, monolithic pro–gun control medical establishment, not to mention the mainstream media.

In a 1986 NEJM paper, Kellermann and associates, for example, claimed their "scientific research" proved that defending oneself or one's family with a firearm in the home is dangerous and counterproductive, claiming "a gun owner is 43 times more likely to kill a family member than an intruder." This erroneous assertion is what Dr. Edgar Suter, chairman of Doctors for Integrity in Policy Research (DIPR), has accurately termed Kellermann's "43 times fallacy" for gun ownership.

In a critical and now classic review published in the March 1994 *Journal of the Medical Association of Georgia* (JMAG), Suter not only found evidence of "methodologic and conceptual errors," such as prejudicially truncated data and non-sequitur logic, but also "overt mendacity" including the listing of "the correct methodology which was described but never used by the authors." Moreover, the gun-control researchers "deceptively understated" the protective benefits of guns. Suter wrote: "The true measure of the protective benefits of guns are the lives and medical costs saved, the injuries prevented, and the property protected—not the burglar or rapist body count. Since only 0.1 percent–0.2 percent of defensive uses of guns involve the death of the criminal, any study, such as this, that counts criminal deaths as the only measure of the protective benefits of guns will expectedly underestimate the benefits of firearms by a factor of 500 to 1,000."

Greater Risk to Victims?

In 1993, in another peer-reviewed NEJM article (the research again heavily funded by the CDC), Kellermann attempted to show that guns in the home are a greater risk to the residents than to the assailants. Despite valid criticisms by reputable scholars of his previous works (including the 1986 study), Kellermann used the same flawed methodology and non-sequitur approach. He also used study populations with disproportionately high rates of serious psychosocial dysfunction from three selected counties known to be unrepresentative of the general U.S. population. . . .

What we do know, thanks to the meticulous and sound scholarship of Professor Gary Kleck of Florida State University and DIPR, is that the benefits of gun ownership by law-abiding citizens have been greatly underestimated. In his monumental work, *Point Blank: Guns and Violence in America* (1991), myriad articles, and his last book, *Targeting Guns* (1997), Kleck found that the defensive uses of firearms by citizens total 2.5 million per year and dwarf offensive gun uses by criminals. Between 25 and 75 lives are saved by a gun for every life lost to one. Medical costs saved by guns in the hands of law-abiding citizens are 15 times greater than costs incurred by criminal uses of firearms. Guns also prevent injuries to good people and protect billions of dollars of property every year.

Recent data by John R. Lott Jr. in his book *More Guns, Less Crime: Understanding Crime and Gun-Control Laws* have also been suppressed by the mainline medical journals and public-health literature. Lott studied the FBI's massive yearly crime statistics for all 3,054 U.S. counties over 18 years (1977–1994), the largest national survey of gun ownership and state police documentation in illegal gun use. He came to some startling conclusions:

- While neither state waiting periods nor the federal Brady Law is associated with a reduction in crime rates, *adopting concealed-carry gun laws cut death rates from public multiple shootings by a whopping 69 percent.*
- Allowing people to carry concealed weapons deters violent crime—without any apparent increase in accidental death. If states without right-to-carry laws had adopted them in 1992, about 1,570 murders, 4,177 rapes, and 60,000 aggravated assaults would have been avoided annually.
- Children 14 to 15 years of age are 14.5 times more likely to die from automobile injuries, five times more likely to die from drowning or fire and burns, and three times more likely to die from bicycle accidents than they are to die from gun accidents.
- When concealed-carry laws went into effect in a given

county, murders fell by 8 percent, rapes by 5 percent, and aggravated assaults by 7 percent.

- For each additional year concealed-carry laws are in effect, the murder rate declines by 3 percent, robberies by over 2 percent, and rape by 1 percent.

Another favorite view of the gun-control and public-health establishments is the myth propounded by Dr. Mark Rosenberg, former director of the National Center for Injury Prevention and Control (NCIPC) of the CDC. Rosenberg wrote: "Most of the perpetrators of violence are not criminals by trade or profession. Indeed, in the area of domestic violence, most of the perpetrators are never accused of any crime. The victims and perpetrators are ourselves—ordinary citizens, students, professionals, and even public health workers."

That statement is contradicted by government data. The fact is that the typical murderer has had a prior criminal history of at least six years with four felony arrests before he finally commits murder. The FBI statistics reveal that 75 percent of all violent crimes for any locality are committed by 6 percent of hardened criminals and repeat offenders. Less than 2 percent of crimes committed with firearms are carried out by licensed law-abiding citizens.

Violent crimes continue to be a problem in the inner cities owing to gangs involved in the drug trade and hardened criminals. Crimes in rural areas for both blacks and whites, despite the preponderance of guns, remain low. Evidence supports the view that availability of guns per se does not cause crime. Prohibitionist government policies and gun control (rather than crime control) exacerbate the problem by making it more difficult for law-abiding citizens to defend themselves, their families, and their property. Prohibition in the 1920s and passage of the Gun Control Act of 1968 brought about an increase, not a decrease, in both the rates of homicides and suicides.

A Sinister Objective

As a physician and medical historian, I have always been a staunch supporter of public health in its traditional role of fighting pestilential diseases and promoting health by educating the public on hygiene, sanitation, and preventable diseases; but I deeply resent the workings of that unrecognizable part of public health that has emerged in the last three decades with its politicized agenda, proclivity toward suppression of views with which it disagrees, and the promulgation of preordained research that is frequently tainted and result-oriented; it can only be characterized as being based on junk science.

In 1996, the U.S. House of Representatives voted to shift $2.6 million away from the NCIPC and earmark it for other health research projects. The redirected money was the amount formerly allocated to the discredited "gun (control) research." Moreover, the House forbade the CDC from allocating further money for that research in the future. Kellermann's gun research was for the first time defunded. Unfortunately, other gun prohibitionist researchers, like Drs. Sloan, Garen J. Wintemute, Colin Loftin, and Frederick P. Rivara, continue to publish their slanted research in the complying mainstream medical journals. They are encouraged in their work by the sponsoring schools of public health sprouting all over the country and funded by the American Medical Association (sometimes through public-private partnerships) or by the large, private statist foundations such as the Joyce Foundation.

Thus the task of separating science from politics is far from over. Much more needs to be done to return public health to its traditional role of stamping out infectious diseases and epidemics—and reeling it back from meddling in politics.

> "Now I think we're prepared to get rid of
> the damned things entirely—the
> handguns, the semis and the automatics."

Private Ownership of Handguns Should Be Banned

Roger Rosenblatt

In the following viewpoint, Roger Rosenblatt argues that private ownership of handguns and assault weapons should be banned. He contends that the myth of the gun-loving American and the idea that gun ownership insures liberty have long prevented any kind of meaningful gun control. However, he maintains that in light of an increase in school shootings, Americans are poised to ban the possession of all guns not used for hunting. Roger Rosenblatt is a contributing editor and essayist for the *New York Times Magazine*.

As you read, consider the following questions:
1. According to Rosenblatt, who invented the enduring image of "shoot-'em up America"?
2. In what country is crime virtually nonexistent despite the fact that there is a gun in every home, according to the author?
3. According to the author, what is the Bell Campaign?

As terrible as [the May 1999 school] shooting in Atlanta was [in which six students were injured by a gunman], as terrible as all the gun killings of the past few months have been, one has the almost satisfying feeling that the country is going through the literal death throes of a barbaric era and that mercifully soon, one of these monstrous episodes will be the last.[1] High time. My guess, in fact, is that the hour has come and gone—that the great majority of Americans are saying they favor gun control when they really mean gun banishment. Trigger locks, waiting periods, purchase limitations, which may seem important corrections at the moment, will soon be seen as mere tinkering with a machine that is as good as obsolete. Marshall McLuhan said that by the time one notices a cultural phenomenon, it has already happened. I think the country has long been ready to restrict the use of guns, except for hunting rifles and shotguns, and now I think we're prepared to get rid of the damned things entirely—the handguns, the semis and the automatics.

Those who claim otherwise tend to cite America's enduring love affair with guns, but there never was one. The image of shoot-'em-up America was mainly the invention of gunmaker Samuel Colt, who managed to convince a malleable 19th century public that no household was complete without a firearm—"an armed society is a peaceful society." This ludicrous aphorism, says historian Michael Bellesiles of Emory University, turned 200 years of Western tradition on its ear. Until 1850, fewer than 10% of U.S. citizens had guns. Only 15% of violent deaths between 1800 and 1845 were caused by guns. Reputedly wide-open Western towns, such as Dodge City and Tombstone, had strict gun-control laws; guns were confiscated at the Dodge City limits.

If the myth of a gun-loving America is merely the product of gun salesmen, dime-store novels, movies and the National Rifle Association (NRA)—which, incidentally, was not opposed to gun control until the 1960s, when gun buying sharply increased—it would seem that creating a gun-free society would be fairly easy. But the culture itself has re-

1. One of the shootings the author refers to occurred in April 1999. Two young males, age eighteen and seventeen, killed twelve students, a teacher, and themselves at Columbine High School in Littleton, Colorado.

tarded such progress by creating and embellishing an absurd though appealing connection among guns, personal power, freedom and beauty. The old western novels established a cowboy corollary to the Declaration of Independence by depicting the cowboy as a moral loner who preserves the peace and his own honor by shooting faster and surer than the competition. The old gangster movies gave us opposite versions of the same character. Little Caesar is simply an illegal Lone Ranger, with the added element of success in the free market. In more recent movies, guns are displayed as art objects, people die in balletic slow motion, and right prevails if you own "the most powerful handgun in the world." I doubt that any of this nonsense causes violence, but after decades of repetition, it does invoke boredom. And while I can't prove it, I would bet that gun-violence entertainment will soon pass too, because people have had too much of it and because it is patently false.

Before one celebrates the prospect of disarmament, it should be acknowledged that gun control is one of those issues that are simultaneously both simpler and more complicated than it appears. Advocates usually point to Britain, Australia and Japan as their models, where guns are restricted and crime is reduced. They do not point to Switzerland, where there is a gun in every home and crime is practically nonexistent. Nor do they cite as sources criminology professor Gary Kleck of Florida State University, whose studies have shown that gun ownership reduces crime when gun owners defend themselves, or Professor John R. Lott Jr. of the University of Chicago Law School, whose research has indicated that gun regulation actually encourages crime.

The constitutional questions raised by gun control are serious as well. In a way, the anti-gun movement mirrors the humanitarian movement in international politics. Bosnia, Kosovo and Rwanda have suggested that the West, the U.S. in particular, is heading toward a politics of human rights that supersedes the politics of established frontiers and, in some cases, laws. Substitute private property for frontiers and the Second Amendment for laws, and one begins to see that the politics of humanitarianism requires a trade-off involving the essential underpinnings of American life. To tell Americans what they can or cannot own and do in their homes is always a tricky business. As for the Second Amendment, it may pose an inconvenience for gun-control advocates, but no more an inconvenience than the First Amendment offers those who blame violence on movies and television.

Gun-control forces also ought not to make reform an implicit or explicit attack on people who like and own guns. Urban liberals ought to be especially alert to the cultural bigotry that categorizes such people as hicks, racists, psychotics and so forth. For one thing, a false moral superiority is impractical and incites a backlash among people otherwise sympathetic to sensible gun control, much like the backlash the pro–abortion rights forces incurred once their years of political suasion had ebbed. And the demonizing of gun owners or even the NRA is simply wrong. The majority of gun owners are as dutiful, responsible and sophisticated as most of their taunters.

Domestic Disarmament

What is needed is domestic disarmament. This is the policy of practically all other Western democracies, from Canada to Britain to Germany, from France to Scandinavia. Domestic disarmament entails the removal of arms from private hands and, ultimately, from much of the police force. Once guns are hard to obtain and the very possession and sale of them are offenses, the level of violent crime will fall significantly.

Amitai Etzioni, *The Case for Domestic Disarmament*, 1991.

That said, I am pleased to report that the likelihood of sweeping and lasting changes in the matter of America and guns has never been higher. There comes a time in every civilization when people have had enough of a bad thing, and the difference between this moment and previous spasms of reform is that it springs from the grass roots and is not driven by politicians or legal institutions. Gun-control sentiment is everywhere in the country these days—in the White House, the presidential campaigns, the legislatures, the law courts and the gun industry itself. But it seems nowhere more conspicuous than in the villages, the houses of worship and the consensus of the kitchen.

Not surprisingly, the national legislature has done the least to represent the nation on this issue. After the passage of the 1994 crime bill and its ban on assault weapons, the Republican Congress of 1994 nearly overturned the assault-weapons provision of the bill. Until Columbine the issue remained moribund, and after Columbine, moribund began to look good to the gun lobby. Thanks to an alliance of House Republicans and a prominent Democrat, Michigan's John Dingell, the most modest of gun-control measures, which had barely limped wounded into the House from the Senate, was killed. "Guns have little or nothing to do with juvenile violence," said Tom Delay of Texas. Compared with his other assertions— that shootings are the product of day care, birth control and the teaching of evolution—that sounded almost persuasive.

A more representative representative of public feeling on this issue is New York's Carolyn McCarthy, whom gun violence brought into politics when her husband was killed and her son grievously wounded by a crazed shooter on a Long Island Railroad train in 1993. McCarthy made an emotional, sensible and ultimately ineffectual speech in the House in an effort to get a stronger measure passed.

"When I gave that speech," she says, "I was talking more to the American people than to my colleagues. I could see that most of my colleagues had already made up their minds. I saw games being played. But this was not a game with me. I looked up in the balcony, and I saw people who had been with me all along on this issue. Victims and families of victims. We're the ones who know what it's like. We're the ones who know the pain."

Following upon Columbine, the most dramatic grass-roots effort has been the Bell Campaign [now known as the Million Mom March]. Modeled on Mothers Against Drunk Driving, the campaign . . . designates one day a year to toll bells all over the country for every victim of guns during the previous year. The aim of the Bell Campaign is to get guns off the streets and out of the hands of just about everyone except law officers and hunters. Andrew McGuire, executive director, whose cousin was killed by gunfire many years ago, wants gun owners to register and reregister every year. "I used to say that we'd get rid of most of the guns in 50 years," he tells me.

"Now I say 25. And the reason for my optimism is that until now, we've had no grass-roots opposition to the NRA."

One must remember, however, that the NRA too is a grass-roots organization. A great deal of money and the face and voice of its president, Charlton Heston, may make it seem like something more grand and monumental, but its true effectiveness exists in small local communities where one or two thousand votes can swing an election. People who own guns and who ordinarily might never vote at all become convinced that their freedoms, their very being, will be jeopardized if they do not vote Smith in and Jones out. Once convinced, these folks in effect become the NRA in the shadows. They are the defense-oriented "little guys" of the American people, beset by Big Government, big laws and rich liberals who want to take away the only power they have.

They are convinced, I believe, of something wholly untrue—that the possession of weapons gives them stature, makes them more American. This idea too was a Colt-manufactured myth, indeed, an ad slogan: "God may have made men, but Samuel Colt made them equal." The notion of guns as instruments of equality ought to seem self-evidently crazy, but for a long time Hollywood—and thus we all—lived by it. Cultural historian Richard Slotkin of Wesleyan University debunks it forever in a recent essay, "Equalizer: The Cult of the Colt." "If we as individuals have to depend on our guns as equalizers," says Slotkin, "then what we will have is not a government of laws but a government of men—armed men."

Lasting social change usually occurs when people decide to do something they know they ought to have done long ago but have kept the knowledge private. This, I believe, is what happened with civil rights, and it is happening with guns. I doubt that it will be 25 years before we're rid of the things. In 10 years, even five, we could be looking back on the past three decades of gun violence in America the way one once looked back upon 18th century madhouses. I think we are already doing so but not saying so. Before Atlanta, before Columbine, at some quiet, unspecified moment in the past few years, America decided it was time to advance the civilization and do right by the ones who know what the killing and wounding are like, and who know the pain.

| "Civilian disarmament empowers not only relatively small-time murderers . . . but also paves the way for major-league mass murderers, such as Adolf Hitler."

Private Gun Ownership Should Not Be Banned

Hillel Goldstein

In the following viewpoint, Hillel Goldstein contends that banning private gun ownership endangers the lives of citizens. He describes his own experience of being shot by an extremist in order to illustrate why citizens need to arm themselves for protection. Goldstein claims that societies that have been disarmed are at the mercy of mass murderers such as Adolf Hitler. Hillel Goldstein, who is working on a doctorate in psychology, was seriously wounded by a gunman in 1999.

As you read, consider the following questions:
1. On what date was Goldstein shot by Benjamin Smith, according to the author?
2. According to the author, what happened to him while he was recovering from gunshot wounds in the hospital?
3. What does the Torah command Jews to do, according to Goldstein?

From "I Am Alive, No Thanks to Gun Control," by Hillel Goldstein, *New American*, July 17, 2000. Copyright © 2000 by The New American. Reprinted with permission.

There are times in our lives when many of our most basic assumptions come under a barrage from the heavy artillery of reality. Some of us receive such a wake-up call in the form of a life-threatening event that literally shatters our lives. It is then up to us to do our best to take inventory of the damage to body and soul, pick up the pieces, and start afresh. I would like to tell you, at the time of the anniversary of a horrible encounter that almost killed me, of such a time of reckoning. But first, some background will help.

I was born in Rochester, New York, on the holiest of Jewish Holidays, Yom Kippur. My parents are American-born children of Eastern European Orthodox Jewish immigrants. Had my grandparents chosen to stay in Europe, I would not be around. During World War II, every member of my paternal and maternal families that stayed behind in Galicia and Lithuania died a horrible death at the hands of the Nazis. So we can be counted among the fortunate ones.

Martial Memories

My family and I moved to Israel in 1973, a month before the Yom Kippur War. At the time, it seemed strange to see young men and women toting rifles. I quickly learned the reason for this: These young conscripts were the first to leap into action if anything went awry. Almost daily, I heard news accounts—terrifying, chilling stories—about terrorists who invaded high school dormitories, or who stormed into the apartments of regular Israeli citizens. Since most Israelis serve in the Reserves until well into middle age, many of them were able to fight back, although the terrorists tended to have the cowardly advantage of sheer surprise. I was drafted into service in the Israel Defense Forces in 1983, and served for three years in a combat unit. I saw two tours of combat duty in Lebanon. By the time I became a staff sergeant, firearms were a natural extension of my arm, reserved for what police marksmanship trainer Massad Ayoob would call the gravest extreme.

At various points in my military career, I carried an M-16, short M-16, M-203, Galil, and short Galil (Glilon). I was a good shot and a disciplined soldier. In my specialty in the Israeli Defense Force, I functioned as a drill sergeant for the

18-year-old boy-soldiers who were recruited every few months. The many stereotypes that abound about basic training stem, in part, from the immensely difficult task that recruits must master within six months: They must transform themselves from high-school graduates into soldiers. The extreme psychological stress inherent in military combat duty left a strong impression on me. I became fascinated with the amazing adaptability of people to less-than-ideal situations. I developed an interest in psychology that has guided my career ever since.

Attacked in the U.S.A.

In the summer of 1986 I returned to the U.S. After acquiring a bachelor's degree and two master's degrees in psychology, I settled in Chicago, to raise a family and complete my Doctor of Psychology degree. I lost contact with the world of firearms—until Benjamin Smith, a neo-Nazi from a wealthy home, tried to kill me as I walked home from synagogue on Friday, July 2, 1999.

I am a Chassidic Jew, and at the time of Benjamin Smith's attack I was wearing my traditional Sabbath garb. "Easy target," he must have thought. Like many complacent Americans, I used to think—naively—that spree-killings such as Benjamin Smith's couldn't happen in "my neighborhood." Yet there he was, my would-be assassin, idling at the stop sign on my block. As soon as I came within a few feet of his vehicle, he opened fire. I didn't have a clue what was happening. As it was the Fourth of July weekend, firecrackers had been going off all day, and this did not sound any different. I kept walking, but I felt a sudden pain and I realized that I was bleeding heavily. I had been shot in the abdomen, shoulder, and arm. And so, on the Fourth of July weekend, when we proudly celebrate our independence, I almost died.

What About Gun Control?

I was categorized as seriously wounded, and, thank God, received emergency treatment at one of Chicago's best trauma units. As I convalesced in the hospital I was astounded at the number of phone calls I received right in my room from the news media, local and national. Suddenly I was "somebody" to these folks, because Benjamin Smith was still on the rampage in Illinois and Indiana, and reporters hungry for a scoop continually pestered me for an interview. I refused to speak to anyone. Although that time is somewhat clouded by a painkiller and IV-induced haze, I recall all too clearly that the vast majority of the media people wanted to speak with me about the implication of my personal tragedy for "gun control."

Firearm Deterrence

We must learn to live with guns, and researcher John Lott seems to be right that we will be better off with more of them in the hands of law-abiding citizens. His argument is like columnist Charles Krauthammer's observation that nuclear deterrence is more stable when two nations have large arsenals of nuclear weapons (the United States and the Soviet Union) than when they have very small numbers (India and Pakistan), because in the former case, any first strike is deterred by the likelihood of a response in kind. Similarly, criminals are less disposed to murder, rape, and rob when they know that their intended victim might carry a gun.

Michael Barone, *Public Interest*, October 15, 1998.

As a result of my experience, I became interested in the issues pertaining to the so-called panacea called gun control, and decided to investigate the question with an open mind. I read about handguns, studied Second Amendment issues, and examined all sides of the argument. To my dismay I reached the conclusion—without any help from such groups as the National Rifle Association, Gun Owners of America, Jews for the Preservation of Firearms Ownership, or the John Birch Society—that good, law-abiding people are being systematically disarmed. While some might contend that my traumatic experience impaired my judgment, I beg to differ: It seems to me that as a result of my personal tragedy I can actually see much more clearly than before. All I want is to have the legal option to have a fighting chance of surviving if a two-legged animal of any persuasion tries to kill me again, or if, Heaven forbid, my beloved wife and two small children are in mortal danger.

Many of the things said in the aftermath of Benjamin

Smith's rampage, and the shooting spree conducted just weeks later by neo-Nazi Buford Furrow, were utterly astonishing to me. Both Smith and Furrow were racist pagans inspired by Hitler's National Socialist ideology; Furrow made a point of saying that his attack on a Jewish day-care center was intended as a "wake-up call for America to kill Jews." Guardians of "respectable" opinion properly condemned the murderous bigotry displayed by Smith and Furrow. However, the "real" problem, Americans were told, was private gun ownership, and the "solution" was to deprive law-abiding citizens of the means to protect their families from violent crime. This was the message of the White House–orchestrated piece of political theater called the "Million Mom March."

Lesson of History

Surely, there are clear lessons taught by history, one of which is that civilian disarmament empowers not only relatively small-time murderers such as Smith and Furrow, but also paves the way for major-league mass murderers, such as Adolf Hitler. It would seem that this lesson would be particularly clear to American Jews. However, I was to learn, much to my amazement, that my newfound understanding of this lesson was extremely unpopular in my very own Orthodox Jewish community.

As I eagerly—and somewhat naively—shared my insights within my community, I was hit with repeated fusillades of empty clichés: "The police are here to protect us" (although they were nowhere to be found when I took three slugs from a neo-Nazi nutcase); "You're not in the Army anymore"; and so on. I soon realized that I had to keep my opinions to myself. I do not mean to upbraid these good people: My community consists of kind, pious, God-fearing people who still adhere to traditional values, and I am proud to be associated with them. They were of great help and comfort to me and to my family during my long recovery at home. But I think they were scared by the new fire in my soul. Like many other good people, their views of the right to bear arms have been shaped by people who seek the destruction of liberty.

My painful experience clarified issues for me. Far too

many of my ancestors died under Hitler's National Socialist reign of terror for me to defile their memory by indifference. A few months after I was shot, I walked into the local gun shop with great trepidation, expecting to meet Jew-hating Neanderthals bedecked in Nazi regalia. Obviously, my own views had been molded, in part, by the same omnipresent, anti-gun propaganda that has had such an impact on the minds of my Orthodox Jewish friends. But of course, the people I met were genuinely nice guys. They were sincerely sympathetic and not at all patronizing when I told them about my experience, and were eager to help—unlike the "compassionate" media people who pestered me in the hospital out of a desire to exploit my tragedy to advance the "gun control" cause. With the help of my new friends in the much-demonized "gun culture," I was able to re-learn the art of soldiering, albeit the civilian version.

Someday, I hope that my friends in the Orthodox Jewish community will come to understand that it is *un*-Jewish not to try to defend oneself. In Vayikra (Leviticus) and elsewhere, the Torah unequivocally commands the righteous to defend themselves. Furthermore, Jews, more than most people, should understand the lethal danger of allowing themselves to be disarmed and therefore at the mercy of the lawless—whether the criminals are thugs prowling the streets or despots haunting the halls of government.

This understanding came to me at great personal cost, and I hope that good people across our nation can learn this lesson in a less painful way.

Periodical Bibliography

The following articles have been selected to supplement the diverse views presented in this chapter. Addresses are provided for periodicals not indexed in the *Readers' Guide to Periodical Literature*, the *Alternative Press Index*, the *Social Sciences Index*, or the *Index to Legal Periodicals and Books*.

Michael Barone	"More Guns, Less Crime?" *Public Interest*, October 15, 1998.
Economist	"Economic Focus: Gun Control and Crime," January 13, 2001.
Jonathan Freedland	"The United States of Arms: It's Time That Americans Got Serious About Outlawing Private Ownership of Lethal Weapons," *Newsweek International*, August 23, 1999.
Glamour	"Kids Gunning Down Kids," July 1999.
Bob Herbert	"Addicted to Guns," *New York Times*, January 1, 2001.
Derrick Z. Jackson	"Very Real Costs of Guns in America," *San Diego Union-Tribune*, August 7, 1999.
Don B. Kates Jr., Henry E. Schaffer, and William C. Waters	"Public Health Pot Shots: How the CDC Succumbed to the Gun 'Epidemic,'" *Reason*, April 1, 1997.
Dave Kopel	"An Army of Gun Lies—How the Other Side Plays," *National Review*, April 17, 2000.
Gary Lantz	"Why Didn't We Grow Up to Be Criminals?" *America's 1st Freedom*, February 2001.
Robert W. Lee	"Dangerous Disarmament," *New American*, June 5, 2000.
Edmund F. McGarrell	"More Guns, Less Crime," *American Outlook*, Fall 1999.
Newsweek	"The New Age of Anxiety," August 23, 1999.
Violence Policy Center	"Unsafe in Any Hands: Why America Needs to Ban Handguns," www.vpc.org, 2000.

CHAPTER 2

Does the Constitution Protect Private Gun Ownership?

Chapter Preface

Arguments over gun control often focus on interpretations of the Second Amendment to the U.S. Constitution, which reads: "A well-regulated Militia being necessary to the security of a free State, the right of the people to keep and bear Arms shall not be infringed." Many commentators attempt to interpret the amendment's meaning by speculating about what the Founding Fathers' views were on private gun ownership.

Defenders of gun ownership claim that the Founders viewed privately owned guns as protection against government tyranny. They quote such notables as Thomas Jefferson, who wrote, "No free man shall ever be debarred the use of arms." Daniel D. Polsby, writing in *Reason* magazine, argues that "no ambiguity at all surrounds the attitude of the constitutional generation concerning 'the right of the people to keep and bear arms' . . . . The Founders of the United States were what we would nowadays call gun nuts." Polsby and others contend that individuals have a constitutional right to bear arms and maintain that gun control is therefore unconstitutional.

Not all critics agree that the Second Amendment renders gun control unconstitutional, however. Even analysts who agree that the Founders intended to protect the right of individuals to own guns contend that they might not have been against reasonable restrictions on that right. Moreover, gun control advocates point out that times have changed since the amendment's writing—as exemplified by the emergence of gang warfare in America's inner cities, for example—and argue that the Constitution should change with the times. Daniel Lazare, writing in *Harper's* magazine, contends, "There is simply no solution to the gun problem within the confines of the U.S. Constitution. . . . Other countries are free to change their constitutions when it becomes necessary. . . . Why can't we?"

No one can ever know for sure what side the authors of the Second Amendment would have taken in the current debate about gun control. However, the authors in the following chapter frequently speculate on the Founders' opinions while deciding whether the Constitution protects private gun ownership.

> "[It is] extremely difficult, if not impossible,
> to construe the Second Amendment any
> other way than to ratify an individual's
> right to 'keep and bear' arms."

Private Gun Ownership Is Protected by the Second Amendment

Dave LaCourse

Dave LaCourse is the public affairs director for the Second Amendment Foundation, which works to inform Americans that the Second Amendment protects their right to bear arms. In the following viewpoint, LaCourse contends that the courts have consistently ruled that the Second Amendment does not grant a "collective" right—a right granted to the states—but an individual right to bear arms. He points out that the Second Amendment is part of the Bill of Rights, which grants rights to individuals, not states.

As you read, consider the following questions:
1. In the author's opinion, why is it clear that the writers of the Second Amendment did not use the term "militia" to refer to the National Guard?
2. Which other amendments to the Constitution does the author point to as evidence that the term "The People" refers to individuals, not states?
3. How does LaCourse's revised version of the Second Amendment read?

Excerpted from "What Is the 'Militia'? And Who Are 'The People'?" by Dave LaCourse, www.saf.org, 2000. Copyright © 2000 by the Second Amendment Foundation. Reprinted with permission.

The Second Amendment to the Constitution of the
United States of America reads that:

A well regulated Militia being necessary to the security of a
free State, the right of the people to keep and bear arms shall
not be infringed.

Gun control advocates declare that this Amendment is
only a "collective right" given to the states, not individuals.
Under this premise, the states could form their own militias
to protect state interests without interference from the national government. In this way, the states could be a check
on the national government's power. Gun control advocates
claim that the courts support their position. If the courts actually back them up, then it would seem that the gun control
advocates would have this debate won. . . .

The current debate [about gun control] centers around
the Framers' use of the "Militia," and "the people." These
two phrases appear to stick out as ambiguous and open to interpretation. Relevant court cases, and several Amendments
to the Constitution are needed to properly define these
terms and formulate the intent of the Amendment.

The "Militia"

The Bill of Rights was ratified over 200 years ago. In that
span of time, the meaning of many words has drastically
changed. What some may consider the militia today may be
far removed from the original meaning. Simply assuming
that the definition hasn't changed in over two centuries is a
very dangerous oversight. . . .

Gun control advocates hammer at the idea that the Militia is an organized entity such as the National Guard. However, the fact that the National Guard wasn't even created
until over a century after the adoption of the Bill of Rights
seriously compromises the idea that such a limited system is
what the Framers of the Constitution had in mind.

To resolve this issue further, one must turn to the courts
for advice. And fortunately, the courts have stated how the
"Militia" should be interpreted, both historically, and today.
In the Supreme Court decision *Presser vs. Illinois* (1886), for
example, Mr. Justice William B. Woods in a bold statement
proclaimed that,

It is undoubtedly true that all citizens capable of bearing arms constitute the reserved military force or *reserve militia* of the United States, as well as that of the states; and in view of this prerogative of the general government as well as of its general powers, *the States cannot, even laying the constitutional provisions in question out of view, prohibit the people from keeping and bearing arms*, so as to deprive the United States of their rightful resource for maintaining the public security, and disable the people from performing their duty to the General Government. [emphasis added]

U.S. vs. Miller

The Supreme Court decision *U.S. vs. Miller* (1939) is by far the most interesting case dealing with the militia. To begin with, only the national government was represented at the trial. With nobody arguing to the contrary, the court followed standard court procedure and assumed that the law was constitutional until proven otherwise. If both sides were present, the outcome may have been much different.

However, since only one party showed up, the case will stand in the court records as is. As to the militia, Mr. Justice James C. McReynolds related the beliefs of the Founding Fathers when commenting historically about the Second Amendment. He stated that,

. . .The common view was that adequate defense of country and laws could be secured through the militia-civilians primarily, soldiers on occasion.

The significance attributed to the term Militia appears from the debates in the Convention, the history and legislation of Colonies and States, and the writings of approved commentators. *These show plainly enough that the Militia comprised all males physically capable of acting in concert for the common defense.* 'A body of citizens enrolled for military discipline.' And further that ordinarily when called for service these men were expected to appear *bearing arms supplied by themselves and of the kind in common use at the time.* [emphasis added]

It is interesting to note that Miller was an individual, and not a member of the National Guard. The court never questioned whether Miller was part of the militia and focused on the type of weapon he possessed. The mere fact that there was a question over which arms he received protection for "keeping and bearing" indicated that the right is for individuals, not the states. Otherwise, the court simply would have stated that Miller had no standing under the Second Amendment as an individual and there would have been no question as to which arms he could keep at all. Any lower courts holding that the *U.S. vs. Miller* case gives credence to the "collective right" theory, and unfortunately a few have, are just plain wrong. . . .

"The People"

A collective interpretation of "the people" as "the states" is crucial in order to believe that the Second Amendment granted rights only to the states for forming Militias. Admittedly, "the people" sounds collective, but does it really mean the states?

In order to find the true meaning of "the people," one must simply read the first Ten Amendments to the Constitution, commonly known as the Bill of Rights. The term "the people" was used in the First, Second, Fourth, Ninth, and Tenth Amendments.

The First Amendment has never been interpreted as giving "the states" the right to peaceably assemble. Nor has the Fourth Amendment been ruled as providing only protection for state officials from unreasonable searches and seizures. Why should the Second Amendment be treated differently?

Finally, the Tenth Amendment eliminates any remaining doubt by reserving powers to, "the States respectively, or to the people." *By listing these phrases separately, the Framers must have believed that these terms were different and separate identities. Otherwise, one of the phrases would have been removed from this Amendment.*

Realizing this, how should we interpret "the people"? The Supreme Court has . . . given several possible answers to this question in *U.S. vs. Verdugo-Urquidez* (1990). In the majority opinion, Chief Justice William Rehnquist, along with Justices Byron White, Sandra Day O'Connor, Antonin Scalia, and Anthony Kennedy ruled that Rene Martin Verdugo-Urquidez (an illegal alien) was not one of "the people" and therefore was not granted protection under the Fourth Amendment. Their ruling allowed the admission of evidence seized in a warrantless search of his Mexican property.

Chief Justice Rehnquist, in his delivered opinion of the

Court, states that regarding the use of "the people":

Contrary to the suggestion of amici curiae [friends of the court] that the Framers used this phrase 'simply to avoid [an] awkward rhetorical redundancy,' Brief for American Civil Liberties Union as Amici Curiae et al. 12, n 4, 'the people' seems to have been a term of art employed in select parts of the Constitution. The Preamble declares that the Constitution is ordained and established by 'the People of the United States.' The Second Amendment protects 'the right of the people to keep and bear arms,' and the Ninth and Tenth Amendments provide that certain rights and powers are retained by and reserved to 'the people.' See also US Const, Amdt 1, ('Congress shall make no law . . . abridging . . . *the right of the people* peaceably to assemble'); Art I, S 2, cl 1 ('The House of Representatives shall be composed of Members chosen every second Year *by the people of the several States*') (emphasis added). While this textual exegesis is by no means conclusive, it suggests that *'the people'* protected by the Fourth Amendment, *and by the First and Second Amendments*, and to whom the rights and powers are reserved in the Ninth and Tenth Amendments, *refers to a class of persons who have otherwise developed sufficient connection with this country to be considered part of that community.* [emphasis added]

In a separate opinion, although concurring with the final ruling, Justice Kennedy believed that:

Asay. © 1997 by Creators Syndicate, Inc. Reprinted with permission.

. . . explicit recognition of 'the right of the people' to Fourth Amendment protection may be interpreted to underscore the importance of the right, rather than to restrict the category of persons who may assert it.

The only reason Justice Kennedy agreed with the final decision is because the search and seizure took place outside U.S. borders. Otherwise, he felt that the Amendments, including the Fourth, would provide protection for an illegal alien.

Even the dissenting opinions of Justices William Brennan and Thurgood Marshall give credence to the individual interpretation of the Second Amendment. *In fact, these Justices rejected the narrow interpretation of "the people" given by the majority.*

Justice Brennan cites that in drafting the Fourth Amendment:

They [the drafters] could have limited the right to 'citizens,' 'freemen,' 'residents,' or 'the American people.' . . . But the drafters of the Fourth Amendment rejected this limitation and instead provided broadly for '[t]he right of the people to be secure in their persons, houses, papers, and effects.'

Both dissenting Justices described "the people" as "the governed." They claimed that by making a person obey our laws while even in his own country, he literally has become one of "the governed" and therefore the protection under the Amendments should apply.

Without a doubt, all of the definitions by the Justices would make "the people" certain qualified individuals, not the states or any other entity. *Whether "the people" is interpreted as the "citizens," "freemen," "residents," "American people," or "the governed," it still remains an individual's right to keep and bear arms.*

By combining the historic definition for the militia, "as all persons capable of bearing arms," and a restrictive definition for "the people," such as "the citizens," the Second Amendment could now read as follows:

A well-regulated Militia, consisting of all persons capable of bearing arms, being necessary to the security of a free state, the right of the citizens to keep and bear arms, shall not be infringed.

It should now be extremely difficult, if not impossible, to construe the Second Amendment any other way than to ratify an individual's right to "keep and bear" arms.

> *"A consistent line of Supreme Court and federal appellate court decisions holds that the [Second] amendment does not concern private citizens."*

Private Gun Ownership Is Not Protected by the Second Amendment

Robert Simmons

Robert Simmons is professor of law at the University of San Diego. Simmons argues in the following viewpoint that court decisions have consistently held that the Second Amendment to the U.S. Constitution does not grant individuals the right to own guns. On the contrary, courts have ruled that the amendment's purpose is to grant rights not to individuals but to states, thereby restricting the powers of the federal government. According to Simmons, other court decisions have ruled that individuals can own guns only if they can prove that they are going to participate in a state militia.

As you read, consider the following questions:

1. According to Simmons, what did the *Cruikshank* decision determine was the purpose of the Second Amendment?
2. What did the court rule in the *Miller* case of 1939, according to the author?
3. According to Simmons, how did the *Hickman v. Block* case decide the "right to sue" question?

One of the most hotly debated issues of constitutional interpretation and application is whether the Second Amendment confers rights to private citizens to own and/or bear firearms. Exhaustive research of well-settled case law answers the question, "No!"

From the middle of the 19th century to the present, a consistent line of Supreme Court and federal appellate court decisions holds that the amendment does not concern private citizens.

The Second Amendment

The Second Amendment is based on Article VI of the Articles of Confederation, which were written between 1777 and 1789. Thus, the concept antedated adoption of the U.S. Constitution.

Article VI provided that "every State shall keep a well-regulated and disciplined militia." No provision was made for a standing federal army. Instead, Congress adopted, and the states ratified, the Second Amendment in 1791. It reads:

"A well regulated militia, being necessary to the security of a Free State, the right of the People to keep and bear arms shall not be infringed."

In 1792, Congress passed the Uniform Militia Act, which required "every free, able-bodied, white male citizen of the respective States"—between the ages of 18 and 45—to enroll in his state's militia.

Within two years, all 15 states had organized militias that met the congressional standards. These militias had limited success. They were somewhat useful putting down the Whiskey Rebellion of 1794 and killing Indians. However, they were completely ineffective during the War of 1812.

Within 30 years of their creation, most militias had been eliminated by their states. Throughout the 1800s, militias were gradually replaced by National Guard formations. Completing the century-long transition, Congress in 1916 passed the National Defense Act, which brought the National Guard under the control of the federal government.

It was not until years after state militias had become a part of military history that gun-use advocates began employing the Second Amendment to claim their "inalienable right" to own and bear firearms. Fastening on these words of the amendment: "the right of the people to keep and bear arms shall not be infringed," these advocates constructed a myth of a constitutional guarantee to individual citizens that endures today. That it is only a myth is attested by an unbroken line of federal appellate court decisions reaching back more than 100 years.

The *Cruikshank* Decision

In 1875, the U.S. Supreme Court handed down its first significant decision interpreting the Second Amendment. In *United States vs. Cruikshank*, the court announced that "the Second Amendment declares that . . . (the right to bear arms) shall not be infringed; but this means no more than that it shall not be infringed by Congress."

The court went on to say that "this is one of the amendments that has no other effect than to restrict the powers of the national government." By construing the amendment so that it restrained only the federal government, the Supreme Court opened the door to states and local entities, inviting them to regulate firearms as they saw fit.

The *Miller* Decision

The *Cruikshank* decision foreshadowed the holding in the Supreme Court's most cited decision on the Second Amendment—*United States vs. Miller* (1939). In this landmark case, the Supreme Court considered the original intentions of the framers of the Constitution.

A unanimous court ruled that unless an individual citizen can show that his or her possession of a firearm "has some reasonable relationship to the preservation or efficiency of a well-regulated militia, we cannot say that the Second Amendment guarantees the right to keep and bear arms."

As the court saw it, the claimant must allege and prove that his/her intent for ownership of a firearm is to participate in the militia. By so holding, the court changed the focus of Second Amendment challenges, from an identification of to whom it applies to a determination of the citizen's purpose in owning or possessing the firearm—a much easier analysis.

The combination of *Cruikshank* and *Miller* decisions authorizes the federal and state governments to disarm their citizens, should they choose to do so. *Cruikshank* contributes to this result by holding that the Second Amendment's prohibition applies only to the federal government.

Borgman. © 1993 by Jim Borgman. Reprinted by special permission of King Features Syndicate.

Miller completes the disarmament authority by confirming the power of the states to create and maintain national guards (militias), thereby removing the only legal basis on which a private citizen could block the federal or state governments from limiting—or banning outright—the ownership and use of firearms.

The *Hickman vs. Block* Decision

Finally, a recent 9th U.S. Circuit Court decision delivered a legal knockout punch to gun advocates. In *Hickman vs. Block* (1996), the court proclaimed its intention to "follow our sister circuits in holding that the Second Amendment is a right held by the state, and does not protect the possession of a weapon by a private citizen."

As if to emphasize the irrelevance of the amendment to private citizens, the court even denied plaintiff Hickman the right to sue on the constitutional issue. Addressing the "right to sue" question, the court reviewed the Second Amendment's historical purpose for protecting ownership of fire-arms, i.e., to provide a well-regulated militia.

No longer, the opinion states, will courts examine the purpose for which an individual desires to own a gun. They (courts) will only hear Second Amendment claims from states, to whom the federal government has denied the right to keep an armed militia.

Long have gun advocates, such as the National Rifle Association and their legislative allies, repeated a myth as their mantra. The strategy of this repetition is apparently based on the maxim that if a myth is repeated often enough, eventually it will be accepted as reality.

As the chilling data reported repeatedly in newspapers and on television reveal, guns in America are as deadly a plague as ever beset Job and his neighbors [who went through repeated calamities, as described in the Old Testament]. There are competent lawyers and legal researchers among gun advocates. Their active collusion or silent assent to the myth's propagation is more shameful, perhaps—considering the human toll—than any other offense charged against the legal profession.

"There are no less than four constitutional arguments against federal gun control."

Gun Control Is Unconstitutional

Joseph Sobran

Joseph Sobran argues in the following viewpoint that there are solid constitutional arguments against gun control. For one thing, nowhere in the Constitution is the federal government granted the right to limit an individual's right to own firearms. On the contrary, the Second Amendment expressly grants this right to all citizens. Sobran also maintains that since individuals are expressly granted the right to life, liberty, and property, they are implicitly granted the right to protect them, using firearms if necessary. Joseph Sobran is a syndicated columnist.

As you read, consider the following questions:

1. In Sobran's opinion, what do "free states" need to be secure against?
2. What did Alexander Hamilton regard as "paramount to every positive form of government"?
3. According to the author, what principle does the Tenth Amendment outline?

From "Constitutional Objections to Gun Control," by Joseph Sobran, *Conservative Chronicle*, June 16, 1999. Copyright © 1999 by Universal Press Syndicate. Reprinted with permission.

In his syndicated column, Professor Garry Wills accuses the gun lobby of "bad scholarship on the Second Amendment." Unfortunately, his own scholarship is open to question. He says the Second Amendment is only "a militia ordinance," adding, "In all the ratifying debates on the Constitution and on the Second Amendment, the right of the individual to possess guns was not once discussed."

Mr. Wills seems to have forgotten that the purpose of the Bill of Rights was to restrain the federal government and to reassure all those who feared that it might someday usurp as many powers as—well, as folks like Mr. Wills want it to usurp.

Security of a Free State

In the first place, a constitutional amendment is not an "ordinance," but a principle. The Second Amendment didn't establish state militias (which already existed). It mentions militias as "necessary to the security of a free state." What did a "free state" need to be secure against? Well, marauding Indians, other states, and the federal government itself, if it should fall into the hands of "usurpers."

Mr. Wills should consult his own edition of *The Federalist Papers*, No. 28 in particular, where Alexander Hamilton envisions the state militias mounting armed resistance to the federal government. Hamilton regards the people's "original (i.e., natural) right of self-defense" as "paramount to every positive form of government," including republican government.

There are no less than four constitutional arguments against federal gun control.

Arguments Against Gun Control

First, it isn't listed among the federal government's powers, either in the body of the Constitution or in the later amendments, after the words "The Congress shall have power to" do such-and-such. It used to be understood that the powers of Congress could be increased only by amending the Constitution, and it has never been amended to enable the federal government to limit the right to keep and bear arms. Notice that this is explicitly called a "right," with no implication that the people may keep and bear arms only by government permission.

Second, the Second Amendment, whatever else it means, clearly forbids the federal government to "infringe" that right. Such a positive prohibition against such a power is much stronger than a tacit presumption against it.

Third, the Ninth Amendment says that the people have "retained" other rights besides those enumerated in the Constitution and the Bill of Rights. What were these unlisted rights? Well, that "original right of self-defense" would surely be among them. If you have a right to life, liberty and property, you have a right to defend them against violence.

Fourth, the 10th Amendment underlines the principle that all powers not "delegated" to the federal government are "reserved" to the states and the people. So the failure of the Constitution to delegate gun-control power to Congress should suffice to prove that Congress has no such power.

Limits on Federal Power

In fact, each of these four reasons, by itself, proves as much. Nevertheless, the Second Amendment was added so that even liberals would get the point. It obviously didn't work.

As Madison said in another issue of *The Federalist Papers* (No. 45), the powers of the federal government were to be "few and defined." The supposed federal power to regulate guns is anything but "defined"; it's explicitly denied.

A Founder Against Gun Control

"The Constitution shall never be construed to prevent the people of the United States who are peaceable citizens from keeping their own arms."

—Samuel Adams, during Massachusetts'
Convention to Ratify the Constitution (1788).

Claremont Institute, 1997.

The plain purpose of the Bill of Rights was to limit federal power. Pursuant to this aim, the Second Amendment ensures that the federal government will never get a monopoly of weaponry, just as the First Amendment ensures that it will never monopolize religion or the press. The framers agreed that liberty depends on popular "jealousy" of government, which has a natural tendency to aggrandize itself.

Liberals usually invoke Congress' power to regulate interstate commerce to cover anything they want to regulate. But if this is what the Constitution meant, slavery and alcohol consumption—both of which involved interstate commerce—could have been banned by simple acts of Congress. But everyone agreed that constitutional amendments were required in order to outlaw them.

Liberals also argue that the 14th Amendment requires the states to respect the same rights the federal government may not violate. But they make an exception, in flagrant bad faith, for the right to keep and bear arms.

"*We must challenge and move beyond the mistaken belief that creating responsible gun laws in some manner offends our constitutional rights.*"

Gun Control Is Constitutional

Charles L. Blek Jr.

Charles L. Blek Jr. argues in the following viewpoint that several court cases have ruled that the Second Amendment does not grant individuals the right to own guns. Responsible gun laws do not infringe on individual rights granted by the U.S. Constitution, he maintains, and are the only way to regulate guns and decrease gun violence. Charles L. Blek Jr. is an attorney and Western regional director of the Bell Campaign (now known as the Million Mom March), a national grassroots organization whose mission is to prevent gun death and injury.

As you read, consider the following questions:

1. According to Blek, what did the Supreme Court rule about the purpose of the Second Amendment in the *Miller* case?
2. What example does the author provide to illustrate that the First Amendment's right to free speech is limited?
3. What federal agency is specifically prohibited from regulating firearms, according to Blek?

For too long, our elected officials have hidden behind the phrase "our Second Amendment rights" in order to defend the status quo with regard to guns. Guns are not the root cause of violence; but their widespread usage dramatically increases the lethality of the violence. The news channels overflow with the tragedies. . . .

Clearly, these issues must be addressed. We must challenge and move beyond the mistaken belief that creating responsible gun laws in some manner offends our constitutional rights.

Misinterpretation of the Second Amendment

The Second Amendment reads, "A well regulated Militia being necessary to the security of a free state, the right of the people to keep and bear arms shall not be infringed." In *United States v. Miller*, 307 U.S. 174 (1939), the Supreme Court discusses the purpose and the limit of the Second Amendment and tells us that the "obvious purpose" of the Amendment was "to assure the continuation and render possible the effectiveness" of our state militia forces (our present day National Guard). The right to bear arms was not extended to each and every individual, but rather was expressly limited to maintaining effective state militia.

The National Rifle Association's (NRA) continuous omission of the "well-regulated militia" language in its literature speaks volumes. It even prompted former U.S. Supreme Court Chief Justice Warren Burger to comment:

> It's the simplest thing: a well-regulated militia. If the militia—which is what we now call the National Guard—essentially has to be well-regulated, in heaven's name why shouldn't we regulate 14-, 15-, and 16-year old kids having handguns or hoodlums having machine guns? I was raised on a farm, and we had guns around the house all the time. So I'm not against guns, but the National Rifle Association has done one of the most amazing jobs of misrepresenting and misleading the public.

The NRA uses our First Amendment right of freedom of speech to repeat their misinformed rhetoric. In comparing First and Second Amendment rights, we all recognize that freedom of speech, as broadly as it is interpreted, still has limitations. For example, we are not allowed to yell "fire" in a crowded theater when none exists. However, if we are to believe the NRA, the Second Amendment grants an unconditional right to individuals to possess arms. The NRA's questionable analysis, prompted Erwin N. Griswold, former dean of Harvard Law School who served as U.S. Solicitor General to comment:

> . . . to assert that the Constitution is a barrier to reasonable gun laws, in the face of the unanimous judgment of the federal courts to the contrary, exceeds the limits of principled advocacy. It is time for the NRA and its followers in Congress to stop trying to twist the Second Amendment from a reasoned (if antiquated) empowerment for a militia to a bulletproof personal right for anyone to wield deadly weaponry beyond legislative control.

History tells us that the Second Amendment is based on the colonists' fear of the military forces sent by King George III to compel obedience to cruel and burdensome laws and taxes. Federalist James Madison drafted a Bill of Rights for presentation at the first Congress. His draft of the Second Amendment was ultimately restructured into its present form in order to place greater emphasis on the militia purpose in dealing with the right to keep and bear arms. Ironically, the New Hampshire convention suggested far broader language—that being: "Congress shall never disarm any citizen unless such as are or have been in actual rebellion." It is indeed significant that our first Congress rejected this broad language in order to adopt the present version with its more restrictive language.

The Correct Interpretation

Our federal appellate courts, in interpreting the application of our Second Amendment, have created a well-settled principle of law—that the Second Amendment does *not* guarantee any individual the unconditional right to own a handgun or to bear arms. Beginning with the decision in *United States v. Miller*, the court held that a firearms statute is unconstitutional only if it adversely affects a state's ability to maintain a militia. Numerous other cases uphold laws that regulate private ownership of firearms, such as *Eckert v. City of Philadelphia*, 695 F.2d 261 (7th Cir. 1982) ("The right to keep and bear arms is not a right given by the United States

Constitution"); *Stevens v. United States*, 440 F.2d 144 (6th Cir. 1971) ("There can be no serious claim to any express constitutional right of an individual to possess a firearm"); and *Quilici v. The Village of Morton Grove*, 477 F.2d 610 (3rd Cir. 1973), wherein the NRA attempted to challenge a handgun ban, and the U.S. Supreme Court, by refusing to hear the case, allowed a lower appellate court ruling to stand that stated "there is no individual right to keep and bear arms under the Second Amendment."

No Barriers to Gun Control

The Constitution contains no barriers to reasonable regulations of gun ownership. If we can license and register cars, we can license and register guns.

Most opponents of gun control concede that the Second Amendment certainly does not guarantee an individual's right to own bazookas, missiles or nuclear warheads. Yet these, like rifles, pistols and even submachine guns, are arms.

The question therefore is not whether to restrict arms ownership, but how much to restrict it.

ACLU, "Gun Control," 1996.

The appellate courts agree—the Second Amendment is completely compatible with responsible gun laws affecting the private possession of firearms. The logic involved in these cases is clear and consistent; however, the NRA attempts to distort the true significance and meaning of the Second Amendment. . . .

Lethal Consumer Products

We must not allow the NRA's distortion of the Second Amendment to distract us from the health and safety risks associated with gun violence. We experience tragedy upon inexcusable tragedy, but fail to recognize firearms as the lethal consumer products that they are. Unfortunately, there are no federal agencies to which we can turn for regulation of the gun industry. The Bureau of Alcohol, Tobacco, and Firearms has no warrant to regulate firearm safety and is not empowered to protect us from the dangers of firearm use. The Consumer Product Safety Commission, the agency charged with overseeing the use and manufacture of most household products, is specifically *prohibited* from regulating firearms in any way. Therefore, we must regulate through legislation.

It is amazing that although we readily acknowledge that safety measures like automobile seatbelts save lives, we are unable or unwilling to connect this same philosophy with the handgun. We all understand that an automobile not only affects the driver but all who are within close proximity of the car. The same is true of a handgun. Therefore, we should no longer allow any regulatory exceptions when it comes to these weapons.

When our policymakers are allowed to misuse the Second Amendment as a shield against supporting responsible gun policy, what are the results? Well, the result is a 15-year old armed with a 50-round magazine, opening fire at his Oregon high school in May 1998, shooting off the entire magazine in less than one minute in the crowded school cafeteria, and killing four and injuring twenty. Simple math tells us if, at the very least, we had laws limiting the capacity of magazines to ten rounds or less that it would have been physically impossible for more than twenty people to have been injured or killed during his rampage. We now know that the two young men responsible for the carnage [at Columbine High School] in Littleton, Colorado, in April 1999 had no difficulty obtaining the high-capacity assault weapons that were used in their rampage.

A few weeks after the Littleton tragedy, I had an opportunity to talk with Tom Mauser, the father of Daniel Mauser, one of the victims in the Littleton shootings. Tom described what happened to his son: "Daniel was in the school library during the lunch period and was confronted with a Tek DC9 semi-automatic assault weapon with a 30-round magazine. The assault weapon was pointed into Daniel's face and then exploded into action."

When will we say "Enough?" We must focus on policies that will reduce the lethality of gun violence rather than continuously lament its deadly results.

Periodical Bibliography

The following articles have been selected to supplement the diverse views presented in this chapter. Addresses are provided for periodicals not indexed in the *Readers' Guide to Periodical Literature*, the *Alternative Press Index*, the *Social Sciences Index*, or the *Index to Legal Periodicals and Books*.

Akhil Reed Amar   "Second Thoughts: What the Right to Bear Arms Really Means," *New Republic*, July 12, 1999.

Robert J. Cottrol   "The Last Line of Defense," *Los Angeles Times*, November 7, 1999.

Amitai Etzioni   "Are Liberal Scholars Acting Irresponsibly on Gun Control?" *Chronicle of Higher Education*, April 6, 2001.

Charlton Heston   "Our First Freedom," *Saturday Evening Post*, January/February 2000.

Wendy Kaminer   "Second Thoughts on the Second Amendment," *Atlantic Monthly*, March 1996.

Dave Kopel   "Our Second Amendment: The Original Perspective," *American Guardian*, July 1998.

Daniel Lazare   "Your Constitution Is Killing You," *Harper's*, October 1999.

Bob Levin   "Casualties of the Right to Bear Arms," *Maclean's*, May 3, 1999.

Nelson Lund   "Taking the Second Amendment Seriously," *Weekly Standard*, July 24, 2000.

Jon Meacham et al.   "I Think the Real Target Is the Second Amendment: Interview with Wayne LaPierre," *Newsweek*, August 23, 1999.

Mark Simon   "Myth of a 'Well-Regulated Militia,'" *San Francisco Chronicle*, July 1, 2001.

Robin West   "Gun Rights," *Tikkun*, September 1999.

CHAPTER 3

Is Gun Ownership an Effective Means of Self-Defense?

Chapter Preface

A teacher was raped by a student one day during her first weeks teaching in Ohio. A writer was stalked by a man who used to live in her neighborhood, forcing her to move. A female columnist was threatened by a mugger on a bridge in Washington, D.C. Women often become victims of male violence, and many analysts are urging them to purchase guns for self-defense.

Ann Coulter, the columnist who nearly got mugged, reasons, "We can't have a world without violence, because the world is half male and testosterone causes homicide. A world with violence—that is to say, with men—but without weapons is the worst of all possible worlds for women." She claims that "without guns I'm what is known as prey." Barbara Goushaw, the writer who was stalked, calls guns "a girl's best friend." She contends that firearms are the great equalizer between the sexes because guns make physical strength irrelevant. Gun advocates such as physician Andrew A. Johnstone—who attended the teacher who was raped—assert that women who arm themselves will be less likely to become victims of violent crime.

Although most people would agree that, generally, women are physically weaker than men, not everyone thinks that guns level the playing field. For example, a 1995 study conducted by the National Opinion Research Center found that guns actually make women less safe. According to the study, in 1998, for every time a woman used a handgun to kill an intimate acquaintance in self-defense, eighty-three women were murdered by an intimate acquaintance with a handgun. Women fare even worse at the hands of strangers: In 1998, for every time a woman used a handgun to kill a stranger in self-defense, 302 women were murdered with a handgun. Based on these findings, gun opponents conclude that firearms hurt women more often than they protect them.

However, other studies can be used to undercut such conclusions. For example, a 1996 study called *Guns in America* found that only 6.6 percent of adult American women owned handguns. It could be argued that it is because so few women own guns that the successful use of guns by women in self-defense is rare. If more women purchased guns, in time, perhaps, more women would use guns to defend themselves than were made victims by gun violence.

In a world where force often triumphs, women can find themselves at a decided disadvantage. Evaluating whether or not guns can "even things up" is made difficult by conflicting studies and divergent interpretations. Yet the debate about guns and self-defense has far-reaching consequences not only for women but for all who are at risk of being overpowered by those who wish them harm.

| *"Criminals are motivated by self-preservation, and handguns can therefore be a deterrent."*

Guns Are an Effective Means of Self-Defense

John R. Lott Jr.

John R. Lott Jr. teaches criminal deterrence and law and economics at the University of Chicago. In the following viewpoint, Lott claims that defensive gun use occurs more frequently and is more effective than the media report. He argues that a criminal is less likely to attack a potential victim when he or she fears that victim might be armed. Moreover, according to Lott, statistics show that using a gun to resist an attack results in less risk of serious injury, especially for women.

As you read, consider the following questions:

1. According to Lott, what percentage of the time that people use guns defensively do the victims merely have to brandish the weapon to break off an attack?
2. What is the probability of a woman being seriously injured during an attack when she offers no resistance compared to when she resists with a gun, according to the author?
3. According to the author, what is a "hot burglary"?

While news stories sometimes chronicle the defensive uses of guns, such discussions are rare compared to those depicting violent crime committed with guns. Since in many defensive cases a handgun is simply brandished, and no one is harmed, many defensive uses are never even reported to the police. I believe that this underreporting of defensive gun use is large, and this belief has been confirmed by the many stories I received from people across the country after the publicity broke on my original study [which investigated the relationship between private gun ownership and violent crime]. On the roughly one hundred radio talk shows on which I discussed that study, many people called in to say that they believed buying a gun to defend themselves with had saved their lives. For instance, on a Philadelphia radio station, a New Jersey woman told how two men simultaneously had tried to open both front doors of the car she was in. When she brandished her gun and yelled, the men backed away and fled. Given the stringent gun-control laws in New Jersey, the woman said she never thought seriously of reporting the attempted attack to the police.

Self-Defense Successes

Similarly, while I was on a trip to testify before the Nebraska Senate, John Haxby—a television newsman for the CBS affiliate in Omaha—privately revealed to me a frightening experience that he had faced in the summer of 1995 while visiting in Arizona. At about 10 A.M., while riding in a car with his brother at the wheel, they stopped for a red light. A man appeared wielding a "butcher's knife" and opened the passenger door, but just as he was lunging towards John, the attacker suddenly turned and ran away. As John turned to his brother, he saw that his brother was holding a handgun. His brother was one of many who had recently acquired permits under the concealed-handgun law passed in Arizona the previous year.

Philip Van Cleave, a former reserve deputy sheriff in Texas, wrote me, "Are criminals afraid of a law-abiding citizen with a gun? You bet. Most cases of a criminal being scared off by an armed citizen are probably not reported. But I have seen a criminal who was so frightened of an armed, seventy-year-old woman that in his panic to get away, he turned and ran right into a wall! (He was busy trying to kick down her door, when she opened a curtain and pointed a gun at him.)"

Such stories are not limited to the United States. On February 3, 1996, outside a bar in Texcoco, Mexico (a city thirty miles east of Mexico City), a woman used a gun to stop a man from raping her. When the man lunged at the woman, "ripping her clothes and trying to rape her," she pulled a .22-caliber pistol from her purse and shot her attacker once in the chest, killing him. The case generated much attention in Mexico when a judge initially refused to dismiss murder charges against the woman because she was viewed as being responsible for the attempted rape, having "enticed" the attacker "by having a drink with him at the bar."

Dramatic News Stories

If national surveys are correct, 98 percent of the time that people use guns defensively, they merely have to brandish a weapon to break off an attack. Such stories are not hard to find: pizza deliverymen defend themselves against robbers, carjackings are thwarted, robberies at automatic teller machines are prevented, and numerous armed robberies on the streets and in stores are foiled, though these do not receive the national coverage of other gun crimes. Yet the cases covered by the news media are hardly typical; most of the encounters reported involve a shooting that ends in a fatality.

A typical dramatic news story involved an Atlanta woman who prevented a carjacking and the kidnapping of her child; she was forced to shoot her assailant:

> A College Park woman shot and killed an armed man she says was trying to carjack her van with her and her 1-year-old daughter inside, police said Monday. . . .
>
> Jackson told police that the gunman accosted her as she drove into the parking lot of an apartment complex on Camp Creek Parkway. She had planned to watch a broadcast of the Evander Holyfield–Mike Tyson fight with friends at the complex.
>
> She fired after the man pointed a revolver at her and ordered her to "move over," she told police. She offered to take her daughter and give up the van, but the man refused, police said.

"She was pleading with the guy to let her take the baby and leave the van, but he blocked the door," said College Park Detective Reed Pollard. "She was protecting herself and the baby."

Jackson, who told police she bought the .44-caliber handgun in September after her home was burglarized, said she fired several shots from the gun, which she kept concealed in a canvas bag beside her car seat. "She didn't try to remove it," Pollard said. "She just fired."

Although the mother saved herself and her baby by her quick actions, it was a risky situation that might have ended differently. Even though there was no police officer to help protect her or her child, defending herself was not necessarily the only alternative. She could have behaved passively, and the criminal might have changed his mind and simply taken the van, letting the mother and child go. Even if he had taken the child, he might later have let the baby go unharmed. Indeed, some conventional wisdom claims that the best approach is not to resist an attack. According to a January 28, 1997 *Los Angeles Times* article, " 'active compliance' is the surest way to survive a robbery. Victims who engage in active resistance . . . have the best odds of hanging on to their property. Unfortunately, they also have much better odds of winding up dead."

The Great Equalizer

Yet the evidence suggests that the College Park woman probably engaged in the correct action. While resistance is generally associated with higher probabilities of serious injury to the victim, not all types of resistance are equally risky. By examining the data provided from 1979 to 1987 by the Department of Justice's National Crime Victimization Survey, Lawrence Southwick, confirming earlier estimates by Gary Kleck, found that the probability of serious injury from an attack is 2.5 times greater for women offering no resistance than for women resisting with a gun. In contrast, the probability of women being seriously injured was almost 4 times greater when resisting without a gun than when resisting with a gun. In other words, the best advice is to resist with a gun, but if no gun is available, it is better to offer no resistance than to fight.

Men also fare better with guns, but the benefits are significantly smaller. Behaving passively is 1.4 times more likely to result in serious injury than resisting with a gun. Male victims, like females, also run the greatest risk when they resist without a gun, yet the difference is again much smaller: resistance without a gun is only 1.5 times as likely to result in serious injury than resistance with a gun. The much smaller difference for men reflects the fact that a gun produces a smaller change in a man's ability to defend himself than it does for a woman.

Weak Victims

Although usually skewed toward the dramatic, news stories do shed light on how criminals think. Anecdotes about criminals who choose victims whom they perceive as weak are the most typical. While "weak" victims are frequently women and the elderly, this is not always the case. For example, in a taped conversation with police investigators reported in the Cincinnati *Enquirer* (October 9, 1996, p. B2), Darnell "Bubba" Lowery described how he and Walter "Fatman" Raglin robbed and murdered musician Michael Bany on December 29, 1995:

> Mr. Lowery said on the tape that he and Walter "Fatman" Raglin, who is also charged with aggravated robbery and aggravated murder and is on trial in another courtroom, had planned to rob a cab driver or a "dope boy."
>
> He said he gave his gun and bullets to Mr. Raglin. They decided against robbing a cab driver or drug dealer because both sometimes carried guns, he said.
>
> Instead, they saw a man walking across the parking lot with some kind of musical instrument. He said as he looked out for police, Mr. Raglin approached the man and asked for money.
>
> After getting the money, Mr. Raglin asked if the man's car was a stick or an automatic shift. Then Mr. Raglin shot the man.

Criminals are motivated by self-preservation, and handguns can therefore be a deterrent. The potential defensive nature of guns is further evidenced by the different rates of so-called "hot burglaries," where a resident is at home when a criminal strikes. In Canada and Britain, both with tough gun-control laws, almost half of all burglaries are "hot burglaries." In contrast, the United States, with fewer restrictions, has a "hot burglary" rate of only 13 percent. Criminals are not just behaving differently by accident. Convicted American felons reveal in surveys that they are much more worried about armed victims than about running into the police. The fear of potentially armed victims causes American burglars to spend more time than their foreign counterparts "casing" a house to ensure that nobody is home. Felons frequently comment in these interviews that they avoid late-night burglaries because "that's the way to get shot."

The Substitution Effect

To an economist such as myself, the notion of deterrence—which causes criminals to avoid cab drivers, "dope boys," or homes where the residents are in—is not too surprising. We see the same basic relationships in all other areas of life: when the price of apples rises relative to that of oranges, people buy fewer apples and more oranges. To the noneconomist, it may appear cold to make this comparison, but just as grocery shoppers switch to cheaper types of produce, criminals switch to attacking more vulnerable prey. Economists call this, appropriately enough, "the substitution effect."

Deterrence matters not only to those who actively take defensive actions. People who defend themselves may indirectly benefit other citizens. In the Cincinnati murder case just described, cab drivers and drug dealers who carry guns produce a benefit for cab drivers and drug dealers without guns. In the example involving "hot burglaries," homeowners who defend themselves make burglars generally wary of breaking into homes. These spillover effects are frequently referred to as "third-party effects" or "external benefits." In both cases criminals cannot know in advance who is armed. . . .

When Crime Is Difficult, Crime Rates Fall

To answer [the question of whether gun ownership saves lives] I use a wide array of data [in my study]. For instance, I have employed polls that allow us to track how gun ownership has changed over time in different states, as well as the massive FBI yearly crime rate data for all 3,054 U.S. counties from 1977 to 1992. I use additional, more recently available data for 1993 and 1994 later to check my results. Gun ownership has been growing for virtually all demographic groups, though the fastest growing group of gun owners is Republican women, thirty to forty-four years of age, who live in rural areas. National crime rates have been falling at the same time as gun ownership has been rising. Likewise, states experiencing the greatest reductions in crime are also the ones with the fastest growing percentages of gun ownership.

Guns Make Society Safer

Guns in the right hands make all good people safer—including people who don't own guns. The higher the number of responsible people who have guns ready to be used for self-defense, the safer the public is. The tremendous degree to which widespread gun ownership makes American homes safer from home invaders is one of the great unreported stories of the American gun-control debate.

David Kopel, *Chronicles*, January 1998.

Overall, my conclusion is that criminals as a group tend to behave rationally—when crime becomes more difficult, less crime is committed. Higher arrest and conviction rates dramatically reduce crime. Criminals also move out of jurisdictions in which criminal deterrence increases. Yet criminals respond to more than just the actions taken by the police and the courts. Citizens can take private actions that also deter crime. Allowing citizens to carry concealed handguns reduces violent crimes, and the reductions coincide very closely with number of concealed-handgun permits issued. Mass shootings in public places are reduced when law-abiding citizens are allowed to carry concealed handguns.

Not all crime categories showed reductions, however. Allowing concealed handguns might cause small increases in larceny and auto theft. When potential victims are able to arm themselves, some criminals turn away from crimes like robbery that require direct attacks and turn instead to such crimes as auto theft, where the probability of direct contact with victims is small.

There were other surprises as well. While the support for the strictest gun-control laws is usually strongest in large cities, the largest drops in violent crime from legalized concealed handguns occurred in the most urban counties with the greatest populations and the highest crime rates. Given the limited resources available to law enforcement and our desire to spend those resources wisely to reduce crime, the results of my studies have implications for where police should concentrate their efforts. For example, I found that increasing arrest rates in the most crime-prone areas led to the greatest reductions in crime. Comparisons can also be made across different methods of fighting crime. Of all the methods studied so far by economists, the carrying of concealed handguns appears to be the most cost-effective method for reducing crime. Accident and suicide rates were unaltered by the presence of concealed handguns.

Guns also appear to be the great equalizer among the sexes. Murder rates decline when either more women or more men carry concealed handguns, but the effect is especially pronounced for women. One additional woman carrying a concealed handgun reduces the murder rate for women by about 3–4 times more than one additional man carrying a concealed handgun reduces the murder rate for men. This occurs because allowing a woman to defend herself with a concealed handgun produces a much larger change in her ability to defend herself than the change created by providing a man with a handgun.

"Few homeowners have enough warning to arm themselves with their own weapons [in order to resist an attacker]."

Guns Are Not an Effective Means of Self-Defense

David Johnston

In the following viewpoint, David Johnston argues that few people with guns in the home successfully use them to ward off intruders, in part because they are unable to arm themselves quickly enough to do so. Another reason that most gun owners never use their firearms for self-protection is that few are trained to shoot the guns accurately in high stress situations. Moreover, Johnston contends that buying a gun for protection actually increases the risk that the buyer or a member of his or her family will be shot. David Johnston writes for the *New York Times*.

As you read, consider the following questions:
1. According to Johnston, how many shooting deaths occurred in the United States in 1997?
2. What examples of high profile shootings does the author provide to illustrate why many people are motivated to purchase a gun?
3. As stated by Johnston, what do most experts claim is the most important factor causing gun violence?

The images are grisly. Gunshot victims surrounded by paramedics rushing to waiting ambulances outside a school, a community center, an office building. Little wonder that people worry that a gunman with an assault weapon and a grudge could loose a reign of terror on anyone, any time, anywhere.

Such incidents reinforce a widespread myth that the number of shooting deaths in the United States is increasing. In fact, the number dropped to 32,436 in 1997, the latest year for which statistics are available, from a peak of 39,595 in 1993.

Guns and Self-Defense

But highly publicized shootings, no matter how rare, can prompt people to buy guns for self-protection, an act that, many experts say, actually increases the likelihood that the buyer or a member of his or her family will be shot.

More often the carnage occurs in thousands of small tragedies too mundane to make national headlines in a country where surveys have indicated that half the households have at least one gun.

"The odds that a home will be the scene of a homicide are substantially greater if there is a gun in the home," said Dr. Arthur L. Kellerman, head of emergency medicine at Emory University in Atlanta, who led a team that studied shootings in Memphis, Galveston and Seattle.

And those homicides will have little to do with intruders. A number of studies have concluded that very few people with guns in the home ever use them to resist an attacker. In one study, fewer than two crimes in a thousand were resisted with a gun. The most likely explanation was that few homeowners have enough warning to arm themselves with their own weapons.

Inadequate Training

Even law enforcement personnel who routinely carry weapons are often inadequately prepared to handle a shooting situation, said Philip Hayden, a retired F.B.I. supervisor who conducted the agency's law enforcement training for safety and survival program at the F.B.I. academy in Quantico, Va.

Statistics on gun use offer cold comfort during what

seems like a summer of high-profile terror shootings. In Atlanta in July 1999, Mark O. Barton, a disgruntled day trader, shot and killed nine people after murdering his wife and two children. In Los Angeles in August 1999, Buford O. Furrow Jr., a white supremacist, opened fire at a Jewish community center, wounding five people, and later shot and killed a postal worker.

Doctors Should Warn of Gun Risks

What advice, if any, can clinicians offer to their patients who are considering the purchase of a gun? Based on criteria for judging whether an association is causal, the evidence from comparative observational studies appears consistent with the inference that owning a gun increases the risk of suicide. Most studies show a moderately strong association, the biological mechanism is plausible, the exposure precedes the outcome, the association has been replicated in several populations, and there is evidence of a dose response (greater risk with more or more available guns). Evidence that a gun in the home increases the risk of homicide comes from only 2 studies and seems weaker; however, these studies offer no support for the view that gun ownership confers a net benefit in terms of protection against homicide.

Based on the evidence currently available, it appears that gun ownership is associated with a net increase in the risk of death for a typical individual. Clinicians might advise their patients accordingly.

Peter Cummings and Thomas D. Koepsell, *Journal of the American Medical Association*, August 5, 1998.

But most people are not shot by anti-social loners, assassins or even by intruders breaking into a home.

Gun violence, experts say, is overwhelmingly dependent on a single factor: easy access to a weapon. "On average, the gun that represents the greatest threat is the one that is kept loaded and readily available in a bedside drawer," Dr. Kellerman said. The vast majority of shooting victims arrive at the hospital as a result of a trivial altercations that turned deadly because the combatants could easily resort to weapons, he said.

Some facts: Most people are not shot with assault weapons, but with handguns. Most people hurt or killed by guns are not shot at schools, offices or their workplaces. In Dr. Kellerman's 1994 study of shootings in Galveston, Memphis and Seattle, nearly half took place on a street or in a parking lot, and nearly a third took place in the victim's home. Seven percent were shot in a motor vehicle and six percent in a bar or nightclub.

Of the cases for which the researchers had information about the relationship, if any, between the shooter and victim, more than a third knew each other. Eight percent were gang adversaries or romantic rivals and seven percent of the victims were shot by a spouse, close friend or family member.

Hard to Hit Target

Another problem with keeping guns for protection is that it is far more difficult to hit a target than television dramas and movies may lead people to believe. Even police officers under the stress of an armed encounter hit their targets with only 17 percent of their shots, Mr. Hayden said. This is true even though most encounters occur at a range of less than seven feet.

In part, the high number of misses by the police reflects new gun tactics taught by law enforcement agencies in response to higher powered weapons carried by criminals. In the past, many law enforcement agencies told recruits to aim deliberately and shoot once or twice. Now, they teach trainees to aim deliberately, but shoot until the threat no longer exists.

The average police officer, Mr. Hayden said, fires only 65 rounds a year in training, a number that is probably far more than most civilians are likely to shoot. Practice shooting and training exercises on computer simulators are inadequate preparation for real situations, he said.

In recent years, the F.B.I.'s training program has gone to greater lengths to provide what experts like Mr. Hayden said was the essential ingredient to successful firearms training— simulated scenarios that build in the heavy stress, confusion and fear inherent in most shooting situations when officers' heart rates skyrocket and their ability to think clearly and act deliberately can diminish.

Mr. Hayden introduced the use of guns that shoot paint

pellets that sting when they hit, and realistic shooting situations involving "armed" suspects in scenarios drawn from actual experience. "It's fantasy versus reality," Mr. Hayden said. "If something happens you say, 'This is how I'll respond.' But unless you're trained, you're not going to respond the way you think you are."

> "*Gunpoint confrontations in which private citizens turn the tables on violent criminals occur with explosive swiftness hundreds, perhaps thousands, of times each day.*"

Defensive Gun Use Is Common

Frank J. Murray

In the following viewpoint, Frank J. Murray contends that Americans frequently use guns to defend themselves in confrontations with criminals. While gun control advocates and gun supporters disagree about precisely how often guns are used in self-defense, Murray claims that even opponents concede that defensive gun use is common. He also reports that U.S. courts are sympathetic to individuals who shoot their attackers in self-defense. Frank J. Murray writes for *Insight on the News*.

As you read, consider the following questions:

1. According to Murray, where do the majority of self-defense cases occur?
2. How many incidents of self-defense occurred in 1993, according to criminologist Gary Kleck?
3. How did the Phoenix police department reward Rory Vertigan for catching a cop killer, according to the author?

C itizens continue to arm themselves as protection against criminals, adopting a simple credo: It's better to have a gun and not need it than to need one and not have it.

Gunpoint confrontations in which armed private citizens turn the tables on violent criminals occur with explosive swiftness hundreds, perhaps thousands, of times each day in the United States. This guerrilla shooting war is almost invisible to the public, experts say, because combatants on both sides have qualms about publicity. While public debate focuses on the danger of citizens defending themselves, the media tend to ignore foiled crimes as unnewsworthy.

Opponents on the issue offer widely varying estimates, citing statistics showing that guns are used in self-defense 180 times a day to once every 13 seconds—a breathtaking number even to the National Rifle Association, or NRA, which culls a handful of such stories for its monthly magazine feature, "The Armed Citizen." Whatever the total of potential victims who actually halt crimes with their own guns—a surprising number of them young women with babes in arms—they are growing in number. Among them:

- Two grandmothers in snowbound Moses Lake, Ore., who repelled an attack on their home by four men;
- A deacon in Apache Junction, Ariz., who wounded an armed robber in his church;
- A man in Brewer, Maine, who shot a robber in his front hallway after being slashed with a knife.

"I'd do it again in the same situation," says Marty A. Killinger, 64, of Oregon, who with fellow "pistol-packing grandma" Dorothy Cunningham, 78, defended themselves from an intruder. "I felt we were probably going to get raped and murdered."

Self-Defense and the Law

In some ways, the incident involving the man in Maine is the most unusual. Not only did robber Michael Chasse, 24, a homeless alcoholic with a criminal record, end up pleading self-defense at his trial, but victim Robert Cohen, a bakery executive, turned out to be the brother of Defense Secretary William S. Cohen. Chasse was sentenced April 2 to 12 years in prison after a jury rejected his claim that Cohen surprised him by drawing a gun and shooting him twice in the chest.

"I saw a man with a gun pointed at me," Chasse testified, claiming the knife fell out of his pocket while he was trying to talk to Cohen. Chasse, however, was inside Cohen's house at the time of the stabbing and shooting. As Penobscot County prosecutor Mike Roberts says, "The defendant would have continued the attack if he had not been shot. Mr. Cohen hit him twice and he stayed down."

Although people often believe otherwise, criminals do not routinely sue citizens who shoot them in the course of a crime. "Extremely rare and almost never successful," says New York state Sen. Michael A.L. Balboni, who recalled a criminal suing unsuccessfully for $1 million after being shot by the owner of an inn he was burglarizing in Saratoga Springs. Balboni studied the topic for a 1998 *Fordham Urban Law Journal* article and was the prime sponsor of a bill passed in the spring of 1999 to block felons from "adding the ultimate insult to injury" by using state courts to profit from their crimes. "There's something to be said about closing the loophole, if only to save people from being victimized twice by having to pay for a defense," says Balboni.

Police departments occasionally lose such lawsuits, however. In one such instance, the New York Transit Authority paid $4.3 million in 1993 to subway mugger Bernard Mc-Cummings for a gunshot wound that paralyzed him nine years earlier while he was fleeing from a robbery. The money was tied up for two more years, until state courts in 1995 rejected a plea to share it with the injured crime victim, Jerome Sandusky, 83.

Most reported self-defense cases occur in the 31 states that allow citizens to carry a concealed weapon. Armed citizens most often use guns against home invaders, store robbers and carjackers. Off-duty police with weapons have used them in self-defense. In 1998, for example, an FBI agent in Maryland shot to death a carjacker who chose the wrong victim, as did three women in Washington—all off-duty police officers.

Private citizens cannot possess guns in Washington, D.C., which has the toughest gun laws in America, but authorities have tolerated cases of self-defense with illegal firearms. When robber Roger W. Green put a gun to the head of the wife of store owner In Doi Choi on July 25, 1997, Choi killed the bandit with a shot to his back. The merchant was not prosecuted, either for the shooting or for illegal gun possession.

The Problem of Reliable Numbers

But anecdotal incidents are difficult to translate into meaningful nationwide statistics. "There isn't any source of information that contradicts the notion that people who use guns for self-protection come out of the event better off," says Florida State University criminologist Gary Kleck, whose studies consistently produce the highest estimates of self-defense with guns—and the most controversy.

In 1981, Kleck found an annual rate of 800,000 incidents, boosted that to 1.2 million by 1990 and doubled it in 1993 to 2.5 million. "The general pattern was that the better the surveys got, the higher the numbers got," says Kleck, describing a nationally representative survey of 4,977 adults that was specific to guns. His numbers average 6,850 self-defense incidents every hour of every day, which gives pause even to Kleck supporters. "Defensive gun use in this country is a reality and all estimates of that number are significant, but numbers high or low don't affect the principle that there is a fundamental right of self-defense," says NRA spokesman Jim Manown.

No Surprise

By this time there seems little legitimate scholarly reason to doubt that defensive gun use is very common in the U.S., and that it probably is substantially more common than criminal gun use. This should not come as a surprise, given that there are far more gun-owning crime victims than there are gun-owning criminals and that victimization is spread out over many different victims, while offending is more concentrated among a relatively small number of offenders.

Gary Kleck and Mark Gertz, *Journal of Criminal Law and Criminology*, 1995.

Tim Lambert of the University of New South Wales in Brisbane, Australia, frequently challenges Kleck's numbers. "There is overwhelming evidence to prove him wrong, but unlike an urban legend we know the source of the claim," says Lambert, who tracks the subject because gun control is a hot squabble in Australia as well. "When a gun is used for defense it is reasonably effective," says Lambert, adding that he believes a Justice Department study that supports an estimate of 100,000 to 200,000 defensive uses a year.

Reliable numbers are a sore point for gun prohibitionists and advocates alike because the self-defense argument has become crucial in the political struggle surrounding gun control. "I think it would have a large bearing on deciding the issue," says Desmond Riley of the Coalition to Stop Gun Violence, which he describes as "the most radical gun-control group" in the nation, seeking to halt all handgun sales and manufacture. "It's one of the key factors that keeps gun control from being enacted."

Risk to the Gun Owner

Critics say it is dangerously foolhardy to pull a gun against a criminal. But unpublished Justice Department figures show the risk is less than the alternatives. Crime victims who use guns to repel an attack are injured 17 percent of the time, less than half as often as crime victims who defend themselves with a knife. "About one-fourth of those who don't resist at all are injured, which means nothing is a guarantee of safety in these situations," adds Kleck.

The Coalition to Stop Gun Violence endorses interpretations of the federal study indicating merely 65,000 defensive uses of guns a year but agrees that's still a lot. Nationwide it would mean gun owners use weapons to defend against violent crime more than seven times each hour.

"We understand people are scared of crime and violence, but buying a gun is not the way to go," says Riley, contending a gun owner is three times more likely to use the weapon against a relative than against a criminal and five times more likely to kill himself with it. "The safety that you feel is an illusion."

But Riley also admits: "It's a frustrating, murky, murky world. They've got a hunk of paper that says this, we've got a hunk of paper that says that. After a while you don't know who to believe."

Don't tell Rory Vertigan it's an "urban myth" that gun owners fight crime. Awestruck Phoenix police declared Vertigan a hero and gave him $500 and a new pistol for catching a cop killer after running out of ammunition in a gun-fight with three heavily armed men.

"When they shot him and killed him in front of me, either they were going to kill me, too, or I was going to kill them," says Vertigan, 27, an apartment manager who works nights as a security guard and has a concealed-weapons permit. "There was no way they were going to turn and run after they shot a police officer. There was no way I was going to turn and run either."

The National Rifle Association gave Vertigan a free life membership. . . .

On March 26, Vertigan accidentally came upon three armed Mexican drug traffickers who had ambushed a uniformed Phoenix policeman in the city's tough Maryvale precinct. Vertigan emptied his Glock 31.357 Sig, firing 14 shots with his left hand during a slam-and-bump car chase that left the killers' license number imprinted on the front of his own car. He wounded the cop shooter and forced the driver of the getaway car to crash. Pursuing police seized the gang—as well as a pound of cocaine "eight balls" they were dealing from their white Lincoln—but not before the 6-foot-5 and 300-pound Vertigan disarmed the wounded driver of a .357 revolver, a 9mm pistol and a 12-gauge shotgun.

"I always felt that if my life was in danger or anyone around me was in immediate danger I never would hesitate to use that gun," says Vertigan. "Unfortunately, that day came."

Although Vertigan was seconds too late to save Officer Marc Atkinson, Phoenix Police Chief Harold Hurtt calls him "one of the true heroes of our time" for standing fast when the trio opened fire on him, too. "He realizes the officer is in trouble. Without regard for his own personal safety, he confronted these individuals engaged in a gun battle. He put his life on the line." Atkinson, 28, left a widow, Karen, and their 7-month-old son, Jeremy.

When Felipe Petrona-Cabanas, 17, got out of the hospital, he rejected a lawyer, confessed and was indicted for first-degree murder, which could bring the death penalty, according to a police spokesman. His friends, Oscar Garcia-Martinez, 22, and Oberlin Cabanas-Salgado, 26, also were indicted for first-degree murder.

"Guns play a relatively minor role in preventing crime but a major role in committing it."

Defensive Gun Use Is Not Common

Tom Diaz

Tom Diaz is senior policy analyst for the Violence Policy Center, an education foundation that conducts research on firearms violence. In the following viewpoint, Diaz argues that guns are used much more often to commit crime than to prevent it. He contends that gun manufacturers perpetuate the myth that guns are an effective and often-used means of self-defense in order to sell their products. Diaz also contends that gun magazines help gun makers sell guns by exaggerating the benefits of owning multiple firearms for self-defense.

As you read, consider the following questions:

1. According to the U.S. Justice Department, what percentage of victims of violent crime attempted to defend themselves with a firearm between 1987 and 1992?
2. What three flaws did the Police Foundation find in the argument that guns have an essential and virtuous purpose in a civil society?
3. According to the author, what percentage of Smith & Wesson's pistol sales in 1995 were reported to have been to people who bought them mainly for personal protection?

Contrary to gun industry hype, . . . unfortunate and wholly unintended consequences happen often when people buy guns for self-defense. Scholarly studies by doctors and public health professionals have repeatedly found that having a gun around for any reason increases the likelihood that a family member—as opposed to a criminal—will be injured or killed with the gun. One study showed that members of families that had a history of buying a gun from a licensed dealer were twice as likely to die in a suicide or homicide as were persons similarly situated who had no such family history of gun purchase. This increased risk persisted for more than five years after the gun was purchased.

The Dangers of Keeping Guns in the Home

Other studies have looked specifically at the narrower question of keeping guns in the home for self-defense. One, published in *The New England Journal of Medicine*, found that having a gun in the home makes it nearly three times more likely that someone in the family will be killed:

> Despite the widely held belief that guns are effective for protection, our results suggest that they actually pose a substantial threat to members of the household. People who keep guns in their homes appear to be at greater risk of homicide in the home than people who do not. Most of this risk is due to a substantially greater risk of homicide at the hands of a family member or intimate acquaintance. We did not find evidence of a protective effect of keeping a gun in the home, even in the small subgroup of cases that involved forced entry.

Another study found that for every case in which an individual used a firearm kept in the home in a self-defense homicide, there were 1.3 unintentional deaths, 4.6 criminal homicides, and 37 suicides involving firearms.

These and other studies have documented repeatedly the enhanced risk that comes from bringing a gun into the home. Even the gun press admits the risk in unguarded moments. Describing the demise of so-called "lintel guns," firearms hung over the door ready for immediate action in frontier times, *Shooting Sports Retailer* noted:

> Today, guns in a home used for self protection are not hung over the door but are more likely in a desk drawer or beside the bed in a night stand. When a child is hurt in a firearm ac-

cident it is often the self defense gun that was found, played with, and ultimately fired by the youngster.

Guns Play a Minor Role in Preventing Crime

But how often do people use guns successfully to protect themselves from criminal acts? Does it justify the damage that comes with guns? Apparently not. Most studies have found that guns play a relatively minor role in preventing crime but a major role in committing it. For example, a U.S. Justice Department study found that, on the average, between 1987 and 1992 only one percent of actual or attempted victims of violent crime, or about 62,000 people, attempted to defend themselves with a firearm. On the other hand, criminals armed with handguns committed a record 931,000 violent crimes in 1992 alone.

One advocate of the value of handguns for self-defense is Gary Kleck, a professor of criminology at Florida State University in Tallahassee. Kleck and his colleague Mark Gertz claim their survey research indicates that civilians use guns in self-defense up to a whopping 2.5 million times a year. Naturally enough, the National Rifle Association (NRA) and the gun industry have widely cited Kleck's work as proof of the value of owning a gun. But Dr. David Hemenway, a professor at Harvard's School of Public Health, dissected the work of Kleck and Gertz in *The Journal of Criminal Law & Criminology*, concluding that their survey design contained "a huge overestimation bias" and that their estimate is "highly exaggerated." Hemenway applied Kleck and Gertz's methodology to a 1994 *ABC News/Washington Post* survey in which people were asked if they had ever seen an alien space craft or come into direct contact with a space alien. He demonstrated that, by the application of Kleck and Gertz's methodology, one would conclude that almost twenty million Americans have actually seen a space craft from another planet and more than a million have actually met a space alien.

Be that as it may, the argument over "defensive gun use," or DGU as it is known in the literature of debate, has a more practical implication than whether one's neighbors have chatted with a space alien. The public's view of the merits of gun control is likely to vary depending on whether it believes that guns have an essential and "virtuous" purpose in a civil society. If good people really do use guns to protect themselves from bad people, people of good will may be less inclined to take this tool of virtue away. But the Police Foundation notes three flaws in the "virtuous use" line of argument:

- *Gun use may take the place of other means of avoiding trouble.* Access to a firearm may encourage some people to be less prudent about avoiding confrontations and may enable or embolden others to escalate confrontations.
- *Readiness to use guns in self-defense may lead to fatal mistakes.* Someone who keeps a gun handy for dealing with intruders and other predators may end up shooting the wrong person.
- *The number of DGUs tells us little about the most important effects on crime of widespread gun ownership.* When a large percentage of households and even people on the street are armed, some may change their tactics, acquiring a gun themselves or in some other way seeking to preempt gun use by the intended victim.

Gun Makers Jump on the Self-Defense Bandwagon

Not bothering with the niceties of whether their products end up causing more deaths and injuries than they prevent, gun manufacturers have churned out handguns full speed ahead, seizing the personal-defense market as a lifeline out of flat handgun sales. Then-president and CEO of Smith & Wesson L.E. (Ed) Schultz said in 1992 that he expected to see growth in this personal protection market. "For a lot of people, the handgun is the last line of defense." And indeed, by 1997, *Shooting Industry* would say, "Concealment handguns and other defensive firearms are the bright spots in gun retailing," and advise retailers "It's time to jump in on the defensive handgun market if you haven't already."

The extent to which this second wave of personal-defense marketing has changed the U.S. gun market was summed up recently by writer Ayoob in *Shooting Industry:*

> I recently was leafing through an issue of *Shooting Industry* (*SI*) from 1971. Talk about a blast from the past! A quarter century later, things have changed dramatically.

In *SI* back then, it appeared that shotguns and .22s were the mainstay of the firearms business. A firearms retailer today knows that . . . that type of shooting market is stagnant at best. The guns that are selling during the sales trough in the industry are defensive firearms, particularly handguns thanks to reformed "shall issue" concealed-carry rules in several states. . . . Defensive firearms, sold with knowledgeable advice and the right accessories, offer the best chance of commercial survival for today's retail firearms dealer.

In another article, entitled " 'Trend Crimes' and the Gun Dealer," the same writer bluntly advised that the industry use fear to sell more guns on impulse:

Customers come to you every day out of fear. Fear of what they read in the newspaper. Fear of what they watch on the 11 o'clock news. Fear of the terrible acts of violence they see on the street. Your job, in no uncertain terms, is to sell them confidence in the form of steel and lead. . . . An impulse of fear has sent that customer to your shop, so you want a quality product in stock to satisfy the customer's needs and complete the impulse purchase.

Marketing and Propaganda

The steady growth in handgun sales to first place in the U.S. market . . . reflects the effects of the self-defense boom. Three-quarters of long-gun owners report that they own their long guns primarily for sporting purposes such as hunting or target shooting. But sixty-three percent of handgun owners report that they own their guns for protection against crime.

In 1995, seventy-five percent of Smith & Wesson's pistol sales were reported to have been to people who bought them mainly for personal protection, and a Beretta executive said twenty percent of the company's $120 million 1994 sales came from the personal-defense market, the fastest-growing segment of the company's business. To help push continued sales in the defensive firearms market, Smith & Wesson opened its "academy" to civilians in 1994, and sent instructors on the road to conduct courses in self-defense, including special classes for women taught by female instructors. The company recently invested $2.7 million to expand the facility to include "new classrooms, tactical shooting ranges and a 20-lane commercial range." A Smith & Wesson spokesman said the company may open similar training centers in other locations.

Aliens and Defensive Gun Use

Since a small percentage of people may report virtually anything on a telephone survey, there are serious risks of overestimation in using such surveys to measure rare events. The problem becomes particularly severe when the issue has even a remote possibility of positive social desirability response bias.

Consider the responses to a national random-digit-dial telephone survey of over 1500 adults conducted in May 1994 by ABC News and the *Washington Post*. One question asked: "Have you yourself ever seen anything that you believe was a spacecraft from another planet?" Ten percent of respondents answered in the affirmative. These 150 individuals were then asked, "Have you personally ever been in contact with aliens from another planet or not?" and 6% answered "Yes."

By extrapolating to the national population, we might conclude that almost 20 million Americans have seen spacecraft from another planet, and over a million have been in personal contact with aliens from other planets. That more than a million Americans had contact with aliens would be incredible news—but not the kind actively publicized by reputable scientists. Yet the ABC News/*Washington Post* data on aliens are as good as or better than that from any of the thirteen surveys cited by criminologists Gary Kleck and Mark Gertz as supporting their conclusions about the frequency of self-defense gun use.

David Hemenway, *Journal of Criminal Law and Criminology*, 1997.

The industry gets plenty of help from the gun press in marketing self-defense. Gun writers push the theme in a repetitive and seemingly endless stream of articles. Selling two guns instead of one to the same customer is better, and three or four, better yet, according to the gun press. Industry writers regularly suggest selling customers several *different* self-defense handguns, supposedly to fit the changing particulars of the situation the customer might find himself or herself in. The customer "needs to know that owning multiple, compatible defensive handguns isn't some BS that a 'gunshop commando' came up with as an excuse to take his money."

GunGames publisher Wally Arida put a slightly different

spin on how retailers should follow up to sell more guns to the same customer after a first sale based on scare tactics:

> We scare them to buy one gun. Now let's get these people shooting their guns and educate them to buy more guns. We should tell them, "Now you have your defense gun, now you need to buy a gun to shoot this sport and another one to shoot this other sport." . . .

Putting sales and profits above all, the gun industry has enthusiastically plunged further into the self-defense thicket. It is making handguns smaller and smaller, and the calibers they come in bigger and bigger. Meanwhile the NRA and its allies continue to press state legislatures to enact "shall-issue" concealed-carry permit laws. And while the gun industry's little money-making machine whirs along, America's gun violence body count continues to pile up.

"*[Allowing citizens to carry concealed handguns] reduced murder by 8.5 percent, rape by 5 percent and severe assault by 7 percent.*"

Legalizing Concealed Weapons Makes Society Safer

Morgan Reynolds and H. Sterling Burnett

In the following viewpoint, Morgan Reynolds and H. Sterling Burnett contend that when states pass laws that allow citizens to carry concealed weapons they experience a drop in violent crime rates. Reynolds and Burnett claim that the right to carry concealed guns does not increase the number of victims killed on impulse during altercations nor does it result in an increase in accidental death. On the contrary, according to the authors, allowing citizens to carry concealed weapons makes society safer. Morgan Reynolds is director of the National Center for Policy Analysis (NCPA) Criminal Justice Center. H. Sterling Burnett is a policy analyst with the NCPA.

As you read, consider the following questions:
1. According to Reynolds and Burnett, how many violent crimes do criminals commit each year?
2. What requirements do most states impose on individuals before issuing them concealed-carry permits?
3. According to the authors, by what percent has the fatal firearm accident rate declined in the last decade?

From "No Smoking Guns: How to Answer Objections to Right-to-Carry Laws," by Morgan Reynolds and H. Sterling Burnett, *Gun News Digest*, www.ncpa.org, March 2, 1998. Copyright © 2002 by National Center for Policy Analysis. Reprinted with permission.

S ince 1986, the number of states in which it is legal to carry concealed weapons has grown from nine to 31, representing 49 percent of the country's population. Should we feel safer?

Opponents of right-to-carry [concealed weapons] laws predicted a sharp decline in public safety because minor incidents would escalate into killings and more children would be victimized by more guns in irresponsible hands. Further, critics claimed that criminals would be undeterred by any increase in armed citizens. Indeed, they claimed that right-to-carry laws would increase crime rather than deter it. Experience has proven them wrong.

What objections do the critics offer?

Objection #1: Citizens Are Safe Enough Without Handguns.

Criminals commit 10 million violent and 30 million property crimes a year. Hospital emergency rooms treat an estimated 1.4 million people a year for injuries inflicted in violent attacks, according to a Department of Justice study.

Since the US Supreme Court and lower courts have held that the police are not obligated to protect individuals from crime, citizens are ultimately responsible for their own defense. Carrying a handgun allows millions to effectively provide for their own protection.

Objection #2: Concealed Weapons Do Not Deter Crime.

In choosing their crimes, criminals weigh the prospective costs against the benefits. If criminals suspect that the costs will be too high, they are less likely to commit a crime. The possibility of a concealed weapon tilts the odds against the criminal and in favor of the victim. A survey of 1,847 felons in 10 states found them more concerned about meeting an armed victim than running into the police.

Their concern is well founded. Victims use handguns an estimated 1.9 million times each year in self-defense against an attack by another person, according to a survey conducted by Florida State University criminologist Gary Kleck. Studies have found that robbery and rape victims who resist with a gun cut the risks of injury in half.

Moreover, a study by economists John Lott and David Mustard of the University of Chicago, published in the January 1997 *Journal of Legal Studies*, examined the impact of concealed carry permits. Using data from all 3,054 US counties between 1977 and 1992, the study found that:

• Concealed handgun laws reduced murder by 8.5 percent, rape by 5 percent and severe assault by 7 percent.

• Had right-to-carry prevailed throughout the country, 1,600 fewer murders, 4,200 fewer rapes and 60,000 fewer severe assaults would have occurred during those 15 years.

• In addition, the deterrent effect of concealed handgun laws proved highest in counties with high crime rates. For example, FBI statistics showed that in counties with populations of more than 200,000 (typically the counties with the highest rates of violent crime), laws allowing concealed carry produced a 13 percent drop in the murder rate and a 7 percent decline in rapes.

• Case Study: Vermont. Vermont has long had the least restrictive firearms carry laws, allowing citizens to carry guns either openly or concealed without any permit. Vermont also has maintained one of the lowest violent crime rates in the country. For example:

• In 1980, when murders and robberies in the US had soared to an average of 10 and 251 per 100,000 population, respectively, Vermont's murder rate was 22 percent of the national rate and its robbery rate was 15 percent.

• In 1996 Vermont's rates remained among the lowest in the country at 25 percent of the national rate for homicide and 8 percent for robbery.

Objection #3: Right-to-Carry Laws Boost Killings on Impulse.

Widespread gun availability was supposed to lead to a "wild-west" mentality with more shootings and deaths as people vented their anger with pistols instead of fists. Yet FBI data show that, as a share of all homicides, killings that resulted from arguments declined. In addition:

• Dade County, FL, kept meticulous records for six years, and of 21,000 permit holders, none was known to have in-

The Effect of Concealed-Handgun Laws on Violent Crimes

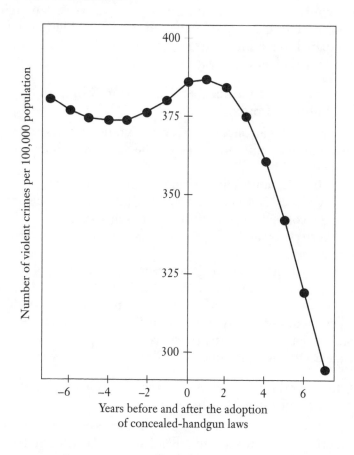

John R. Lott Jr., *More Guns, Less Crime: Understanding Crime and Gun-Control Laws*, 1998.

jured an innocent person.

• Since Virginia passed a right-to-carry law, more than 50,000 permits have been issued, not one permit holder has been convicted of a crime and violent crime has dropped.

Moreover, those who have broken the rules have lost their privilege to carry a gun.

• Texas has revoked or suspended nearly 300 permits for minor violations like failure to conceal or carrying a gun in a bar.

• Between 1987 and 1995, Florida issued nearly 300,000 permits, but revoked only 19 because the permit holder had committed a crime. That's one crime per 14,000 permit holders during a nine-year period, an incredibly low rate compared to a criminal arrest rate of one per 14 Americans age 15 and older each year.

Objection #4: Concealed Carry Puts Guns in Untrained Hands.

Before issuing a concealed carry permit, most states require that the applicant prove he or she has been thoroughly trained, with:
• 10 to 15 hours emphasizing conflict resolution.
• A pre-test and a final test covering the laws of self-defense and the consequences of misuse of deadly force.
• A stress on gun safety in the classroom and on the firing range.
• A stringent shooting accuracy test which applicants must pass each time they renew their permit.

Of course, a person who has only a split second to decide whether to use deadly force can make a mistake. However, only about 30 such mistaken civilian shootings occur nationwide each year. The police kill in error three times as often.

Objection #5: Concealed Carry Increases Accidental Gun Deaths.

The Lott-Mustard study found no increase in accidental shootings in counties with "shall issue" right-to-carry laws, where authorities have to issue the permit to all who meet the criteria. Nor have other studies. Nationally, there are about 1,400 accidental firearms deaths each year—far fewer than the number of deaths attributable to medical errors or automobile accidents. The national death rate from firearms has declined even while firearm ownership has almost doubled in the last 20 years, and 22 more states have liberalized right-to-carry laws:
• The fatal firearm accident rate has declined to about .5 per 100,000 people—a decrease of more than 19 percent in the last decade.
• The number of fatal firearms-related accidents among

children fell to an all-time low of 185 in 1994, a 64 percent decline since 1975.

Concealed carry laws have not contributed to a big increase in gun ownership. Nor has allowing citizens the right to carry firearms for self-protection led to the negative consequences claimed by critics. In fact, these laws have lowered violent crime rates and increased the general level of knowledge concerning the rights, responsibilities and laws of firearm ownership.

Putting unarmed citizens at the mercy of armed and violent criminals was never a good idea. Now that the evidence is in, we know that concealed carry is a social good.

VIEWPOINT

6

"Allowing more people to carry concealed handguns does not mean less crime."

Legalizing Concealed Weapons Does Not Make Society Safer

Handgun Control, Inc.

Handgun Control, Inc., the nation's largest citizens' gun control lobbying organization, argues in the following viewpoint that states should not make it easier for citizens to carry concealed weapons because such measures will not reduce crime. The organization claims that violent crime and robbery rates have declined far more dramatically in states that strictly monitor or forbid the carrying of concealed weapons compared to states with lax carrying concealed weapons laws (CCW). In fact, some states with lax CCW laws actually experienced an increase in violent crime.

As you read, consider the following questions:

1. According to the FBI, by what percentage did the overall crime rate drop during the period from 1997 to 1998?
2. According to Handgun Control, Inc., what percentage difference was there in the reduction of violent crime rates between states that had strict concealed-carry laws and states with lax concealed-carry laws?
3. What percentage of "shall issue" states experienced an increase in violent crime between 1992 and 1998, according to the organization?

From "Concealed Truth: Concealed Weapons Laws and Trends in Violent Crime in the United States," by Handgun Control, Inc., www.handguncontrol.org, October 22, 1999. Copyright © 1999 by the Brady Campaign to Prevent Gun Violence. Reprinted with permission.

An analysis conducted by The Brady Center to Prevent Gun Violence, comparing the latest drop in crime rates among the states, provides compelling evidence that the gun lobby is wrong: allowing more people to carry concealed handguns does not mean less crime. According to the Federal Bureau of Investigation's (FBI) Uniform Crime Reports, from 1997 to 1998 the nation's overall crime rate dropped 6.4%, from 4930.0 to 4615.5 crimes per 100,000 population. More telling is this continuing trend where crime fell faster in states that have strict carrying concealed weapons (CCW) laws or that do not allow the carrying of concealed weapons at all than in states which have lax CCW laws. This strongly suggests that, contrary to the arguments made by the National Rifle Association (NRA) and others, states should not make it easier for citizens to carry concealed weapons in order to reduce crime.

Carrying Concealed Weapons Does Not Reduce Crime

From 1992 to 1998 (the last six years for which data exists), the violent crime rate in the strict and no-issue states fell 30% while the violent crime rate for the 11 states that had liberal CCW laws (where law enforcement must issue CCW licenses to almost all applicants) during this entire period dropped only 15%. Nationally, the violent crime rate fell 25%. The decline in the crime rate of strict licensing and no-carry states was twice that of states with lax CCW systems, indicating that there are more effective ways to fight crime than to encourage more people to carry guns. New York and California—the two most populous states and ones with strict CCW licensing laws—experienced dramatic decreases in violent crime over the six-year period. New York experienced a 43% decline and California experienced a 37% decline, both without putting more concealed handguns on their streets.

Additionally, the robbery rate also fell faster in states with strict carry laws. Our analysis found that between 1992 and 1998, the robbery rate in strict and no-issue states fell 44% while the robbery rate for the 11 states with liberal CCW laws during this entire period dropped 24%. Nationally, the robbery rate fell 37%. Again, New York and California—the two most populous states and ones with strict CCW licensing laws—experienced dramatic decreases over the six-year period. New York experienced a 55% drop in the robbery rate and California experienced a 50% drop in the robbery rate.

In the 29 states that had lax CCW laws during 1997 and 1998, the crime rate fell 6%, from 5296.6 to 4971.2 crimes per 100,000 population. During the same time period, in the 21 states and the District of Columbia with strict carry laws or which don't allow the carrying of concealed weapons at all, the crime rate fell 7%, from 4613.7 to 4297.2 crimes per 100,000 population. While the rate of violent crime for states with strict carry laws fell at relatively the same rate as less restrictive states from 1997 to 1998 (8% and 7.5% respectively), the robbery rate for these 22 strict states fell 13%, compared to the lax states' 10% (this includes an 11% drop for those states which relaxed their CCW laws after 1992, and a drop of only 7% who have had lax CCW laws since before 1992).

"These numbers demonstrate what we've been saying all along," said Sarah Brady, chair of The Brady Center to Prevent Gun Violence and The Brady Campaign to Prevent Gun Violence, Inc. "We don't need to make it easier for just anyone to carry a gun nor do we need more concealed handguns on our streets to fight crime. The way to fight crime is to punish criminals and to make sure that criminals don't get guns in the first place."

The Lott-Mustard Study

The decision to liberalize concealed carry laws by a number of state legislatures was based largely on findings drawn from one study authored by [economist] John Lott and David Mustard [formerly of the University of Chicago]. Lott and Mustard claim that greatly easing restrictions on carrying concealed handguns will lead to a large decrease in crime. When first presented, Lott and Mustard's work was met with skepticism in the research community. Now, a growing body of empirical evidence has completely undermined the credibility of their claims.

Perhaps most compelling is the fact that robbery has declined twice as quickly in states with strict licensing or that do not allow concealed carrying at all than in states with lax CCW systems. If carrying concealed weapons reduces crime, it would be expected that the greatest effects would be seen on crimes that most often occur between strangers in public places, such as robbery. However, Lott and Mustard found virtually no beneficial effects from liberalizing the carrying of concealed weapons on robbery. As indicated above, robbery in restrictive CCW states fell twice as fast as in lax CCW states. Furthermore, reanalysis of Lott and Mustard's data by two different teams of researchers revealed that crime overall was just as likely to increase as decrease after states eased their carry laws—a finding which appears to be borne out by the FBI's crime data.

Turtil. © 1986 by Steve Turtil. Reprinted by permission.

Between 1992 and 1998, over a quarter (27%, 3/11) of the states that were "shall issue" during this entire time period experienced an increase in the violent crime rate, as well as in the robbery rate. This compares to increases in violent crime over the same 6 year time period in just 18% (4/22) of states with strict carry laws. Only 18% (4/22) of states with strict carry laws experienced an increase in robberies. If allowing more people to carry concealed handguns is supposed to be such an effective crime fighting strategy, why did the crime rate go up in so many "shall issue" states—particularly when compared to states that employed other strategies to fight crime? . . .

Law Enforcement and Concealed Weapons

Lax or "shall issue" CCW laws require law enforcement to issue CCW licenses to virtually anyone who is not a convicted felon. In these states, local law enforcement has almost no discretion in issuing these licenses and, in many cases, getting a license requires little or no safety training or even a demonstration that the applicant knows how to use a gun. States that give law enforcement discretion in issuing licenses (so-called "may issue" states) or which prohibit the carrying of concealed weapons entirely have chosen other strategies to fight crime, resulting in the greatest decreases in crime over the past six years.

For several years now, the National Rifle Association and others have made it a priority to get state legislatures to pass lax CCW laws. They claim that putting more guns on our streets reduces crime, despite the fact that almost every major law enforcement organization in the country opposes lax CCW laws. . . .

"[The] numbers should make everyone question the NRA's campaign for lax CCW laws under the guise of fighting crime," said Mrs. Brady. "If the gun lobby is truly interested in reducing crime, they should work for common sense measures like stopping criminals from getting guns at gun shows and limiting handgun sales to one per person per month to cut gun trafficking. Working with lawmakers, law enforcement, the public health community and civic leaders on proven crime-fighting strategies, we can make America safer for everyone."

Periodical Bibliography

The following articles have been selected to supplement the diverse views presented in this chapter. Addresses are provided for periodicals not indexed in the *Readers' Guide to Periodical Literature*, the *Alternative Press Index*, the *Social Sciences Index*, or the *Index to Legal Periodicals and Books*.

Jane E. Brody	"In Repeated Studies, Guns Turn Out to Be 'Protection' That Puts Families at Risk," *New York Times*, May 21, 1997.
Gia Fenoglio	"You've Got to Have a Way of Defending Yourself," *National Journal*, July 22, 2000.
Frederick V. Guterl	"Gunslinging in America: Does a Gun Make You Safer or Increase Your Likelihood of Violent Death?" *Discover*, May 1996.
Handgun Control, Inc.	"Guns in the Home," www.handguncontrol.org, 2000.
Bronwyn Jones	"Arming Myself with a Gun Is Not the Answer," *Newsweek*, May 22, 2000.
Don B. Kates Jr.	"Making a Case for Gun Ownership: Israeli-U.S. Contrasts," *Christian Science Monitor*, December 16, 1997.
David Kopel	"Burglary and the Armed Homestead," *Chronicles*, January 1998.
John R. Lott Jr.	"One Case for Guns: Dramatic Cases of Guns Used for Self-Defense Go Unreported," *Christian Science Monitor*, August 21, 2000.
Michael P. Lucas	"Out There: Gay Firearms Group Takes Aim at Stereotypes," *Los Angeles Times*, July 14, 2001.
Mother Jones	"Who We Kill," March/April 1996.
Romesh Ratnesar	"Should You Carry a Gun?" *Time*, July 6, 1998.
Sheldon Rishman	"The Seen and Unseen in Gun Control," *Freeman*, October 1998.
Thomas Sowell	"Firing Gun Control Hypocrisy," *Washington Times*, June 4, 2000.
Jacob Sullum and Michael W. Lynch	"Cold Comfort," *Reason*, January 2000.
Douglas Weil	"Carrying Concealed Guns Is Not the Solution," www.IntellectualCapital.com, March 26, 1998.

CHAPTER 4

What Measures Would Reduce Gun Violence?

Chapter Preface

On Mother's Day 2000, over one hundred thousand mothers assembled in Washington, D.C., calling for stricter gun control. The marchers demanded that legislators enact laws to prevent school shootings and other gun tragedies that were claiming the lives of the nation's children. They pointed out that "since the assassinations of Martin Luther King Jr. and Robert Kennedy in 1968, over one million Americans have been killed by firearms." The rally garnered much media attention and helped generate public support for the organizers' goals.

The Million Mom March is just one of many campaigns working to strengthen America's gun laws. Numerous organizations oppose gun control, however, the most notable being the National Rifle Association (NRA), which, with over 3 million members, is the nation's largest organization of gun owners. Although columnist E.J. Dionne Jr. considered the Million Mom March a "countervailing force" to the National Rifle Association, the Moms acknowledged how difficult it is to counter the influence of the NRA. In fact, many working for the campaign accused the Republican Party of being in the gun lobby's "back pocket."

For its part, the NRA quickly published rebuttals to the Million Moms' claims. To begin with, the organization refuted the Moms' claim to be a grass-roots campaign. The NRA pointed out that the groups' founder, Donna Dees-Thomases, was a former CBS publicist, and that many of its most active supporters were politicians or celebrities. The NRA also asserted that the "children" whom the Moms were memorializing were in actuality 17-, 18-, and 19-year-olds killed in gang or drug wars. Perhaps the NRA's most vociferous attack against the Million Moms campaign was the assertion that the marchers wanted to strip citizens of their constitutional right to own firearms. Because of the NRA's influence, its claims discredited the Million Mom March in the eyes of many Americans.

In the final analysis, the likelihood of stricter gun control laws being enacted depends in large measure on which national organizations succeed in convincing representatives in

Congress to adopt their views. Such organizations try to influence politicians with campaign donations, media blitzes, and rallies. These activities cost money, and, not surprisingly, the organizations with the most money tend to have the most political clout. The fate of gun control—irrespective of violent crime studies and court decisions on the right of citizens to bear arms—is ultimately in the hands of politicians and the lobbyist groups that influence them.

*"Handguns . . . [make] it possible to settle
with finality the passionate domestic
arguments and street disputes that produce
most of our homicides."*

Gun Control Will Reduce Lethal Crime

Richard Harwood

In the following viewpoint, Richard Harwood contends that
eliminating handguns would reduce America's murder rate.
According to Harwood, America has approximately the
same amount of crime as other Western nations, but what
sets the United States apart is a much higher rate of lethal
crime. He argues that making handguns less available would
decrease the likelihood that commonplace arguments and
disputes would end fatally. Richard Harwood was an editor
and ombudsman for the *Washington Post*.

As you read, consider the following questions:
1. How many americans have died since 1980 at the hands
   of other Americans, according to Harwood?
2. What actions have politicians taken in a futile attempt to
   reduce violent crime, as stated by the author?
3. Why is murder a serious problem, in Harwood's
   opinion?

Excerpted from "America's Unchecked Epidemic," by Richard Harwood,
Washington Post National Weekly Edition, December 8, 1997. Copyright © 1997
by The Washington Post Writers Group. Reprinted with permission.

Americans have invested a great deal of wealth and effort in this century to keep death at bay, and they have had a lot of success. Cholera, smallpox, typhoid have been eliminated in this country. Other diseases that once killed millions now are cured easily or prevented. The average American's life span has been extended by nearly 30 years.

Health and medical care have become our leading industry. We spend more on these services than we spend for food, housing, automobiles, clothes or education.

The Violence Epidemic

But neither money nor science has brought us any closer to solving or even moderating one epidemic in American life: violence. For at least a century and probably longer we have been the most murderous "developed" society on earth. Since 1980 nearly 400,000 Americans have died at the hands of fellow citizens—more than the number of Americans who died on the battlefields of World War I and World War II combined. It would take eight Vietnams to fill as many graves.

Our propensity to violence cannot be explained by the cliche that America is a uniquely "lawless" society. Franklin Zimring and Gordon Hawkins of the University of California write: "The reported rates [per 100,000 people] of both violent and nonviolent crime in the United States . . . are quite close to those found in countries like Australia, Canada and New Zealand." The rate of criminal assault is higher in those countries than here. In robberies, the United States is second to Poland and similar in rate to Italy, Australia, Czechoslovakia, Canada and England. Scandinavian robbery rates are not strikingly lower than those in this country. A study in 1992 revealed that London had a higher overall crime rate than New York City, including 66 percent more thefts and 57 percent more burglaries. But New York has 11 times as many murders.

So it is not crime that sets us apart. We have no more pickpockets, shoplifters, burglars, robbers or brawlers than Western Europe or the British Isles. But we have a surplus of killers—a large surplus. Our homicide rate is 20 times the rate in England and Wales, 10 times the rate in France and Germany and is exceeded only by a few Latin American countries, notably Colombia, Mexico and Brazil.

Why this is so is a mystery to medical scientists (psychiatrists and psychologists included) and to anthropologists and social scientists as well. Politicians have no answers. They wage futile "wars" on crime, expand the police forces and the offenses punishable by death, keep a million citizens in prison, beef up law enforcement agencies and equip them with everything from tanks to helicopter gunships. Through it all, the homicide rate remains almost constant—roughly eight to 10 murders for every 100,000 people in the course of a year.

Rules of the Road

The government has a responsibility to its citizens to limit access to certain types of firearms, as well as to set the parameters under which its citizens may exercise their Second Amendment rights. An analogous example commonly cited is that of the restrictions placed on owning and operating a motor vehicle. Cars are registered and licensed, just as are their operators. "Rules of the road" stipulate how a driver may use his or her vehicle. These rules place limitations on drivers, not as a punishment, but as a way to ensure the welfare and safety of travelers. While the "rules of the road" may vary from state to state, they are largely consistent in order to make the roads of the nation safe. Obviously, these rules are sometimes broken, and people are injured and killed. And sometimes they may seem not to apply, such as the rule that requires a stop at a red light at 2 A.M. when no other car is in sight. Yet we would be far worse off without them. Sensible regulation of firearms is just as reasonable.

Michael W. Warfel, *America*, April 15, 2000.

When 20,000 to 25,000 people are being murdered every year, you've got a problem. It's not a huge problem in the context of death in America; more than 2.25 million of us die every year from all causes—including 30,000 to 40,000 from AIDS, 40,000 or so in automobile accidents and about 30,000 as a result of suicide.

But even in that context, murder is a serious problem. It poisons society with fear and suspicion, turns large areas of our cities into combat zones and contributes to urban flight.

Still, despite our cowboy image in much of the world, it is irrational to assume that a propensity for murder is rampant in the American character; 99.99 percent of us never murder anyone. And there is no uniformity among those who do. Some regions have more violent traditions than others, the South in particular: Louisiana's murder rate today is 20 times the rate in Vermont. Men are more murderous than women. Cities have proportionately more murders than suburbs and rural areas. The 20 largest U.S. cities have 11.5 percent of the American population but account for 34 percent of the reported homicides. African Americans, heavily concentrated in these cities, are at far more risk of death by homicide than nonblacks. They are 13 percent of the American population, but they account for 45 percent of homicide victims and 55 percent of suspects charged with homicide, according to calculations by Zimring and Hawkins. Many theories are offered to explain the relatively high level of lethal violence in these urban communities, but none has been validated. Whatever the "causal" factors, the number and percentage of blacks charged with homicide in the age groups most prone to violence—15 to 34—is tiny, roughly a tenth of one percent. And if black homicides were ignored in the calculations, the U.S. homicide rate still would be three to five times greater than the rates in Europe and Britain.

Handguns Are the Problem

Zimring and Hawkins conclude that the one "causal" factor that sets us apart from the rest of the world is the huge arsenal of handguns—estimated at from 50 million to 70 million—that makes it possible to settle with finality the passionate domestic arguments and street disputes that produce most of our homicides. Eliminating handguns would not eliminate rage or conflict but certainly would lower the life-threatening consequences of these encounters.

People will argue that other deadly weapons—knives, blunt instruments, poison and the noose—will remain available to people who want to kill. Sure. They're available all over the world, too, but nowhere else is murder so commonplace.

It would take political courage to do anything about the gun problem, and it is in short supply in Washington. But no other remedy—medical, chemical, technological or spiritual—is at hand or even on the horizon.

| *"There is an ever-increasing amount of evidence that gun control is a failure."*

Gun Control Will Not Reduce Violent Crime

Samuel Francis

Samuel Francis, a syndicated columnist, argues in the following viewpoint that gun control around the world has failed. For example, he claims that Japan, Australia, and Great Britain have experienced rising crime rates despite passing draconian gun laws. In contrast, Francis asserts that the United States—which does not have strict gun laws—has experienced a decrease in violent crime rates, partly due to the fact that many American citizens are allowed to carry concealed weapons for self-defense.

As you read, consider the following questions:
1. According to Francis, what is the "yakuza"?
2. By what percentage have homicides in Australia increased since that country confiscated all handguns, as stated by the author?
3. According to the author, by what percentage did the number of robberies increase in Great Britain after it banned privately owned handguns?

The most recent crusades for gun control seem to have fizzled, and that's just as well, not only for the sake of the freedom and safety of most Americans, but also for the public reputations of those who push the banning of firearms. There is an ever-increasing amount of evidence that gun control is a failure, not only in the United States but in other countries, too.

Japan

The ancient and honorable nation of Japan has the distinction of enjoying perhaps the most rigorous gun-control laws in the world outside of Communist states. With no tradition of individual liberty and a powerful tradition of placing the integrity of the group—family and nation—over the individual, Japanese lawmakers have never felt the slightest hesitation in outlawing most gun ownership and punishing severely those who break the laws.

In Japan, even possessing a handgun and a bullet puts you in prison for 15 years. Other laws have been tightened and toughened since 1991, and even armored car guards don't carry firearms. Only police officers and soldiers can carry guns at all, and the cops have to leave their guns in a safe when they leave work.

According to gun-control dogmas, that should pretty much keep gun violence down. But it doesn't, in Japan anymore than in this country. *The Washington Post* recently carried a report on the increasing incidence of gun violence in the Land of the Rising Gun.

The number of crimes committed with handguns last year was higher than in any year since records have been kept, and the rate this year threatens to be even higher. An administrator in Japan's National Police Agency told the *Post*, "Since 1994 or 1995 there's been a clear change; the guns are now becoming dispersed in the population. We are worried about it. Crimes are becoming more violent, more serious. And handguns are very efficient weapons for that." So much for the effectiveness of gun control.

The people in Japan who do have guns are the members of the "yakuza," as the Japanese organized crime cartel is known. As the *Post* reports: "The yakuza are the exception.

Experts believe most of the estimated 80,000 underworld members have weapons, and police have been unable or unwilling to dent that figure." Does that remind you of anything? When guns are outlawed, only outlaws will have guns.

Australia and Great Britain

Japan, however, is not the only gun-controlling society to sport rising gun violence. The same is true in Australia, where a new law last year confiscated virtually all handguns in the country and destroyed them. It doesn't matter. Now violent crimes committed by guns are on the rise Down Under.

Defying Credibility

If a murderer intends to break a law against murder, why would he have any more respect for a law prohibiting him from possessing a gun? It defies credibility that murderers, rapists, burglars, thieves, and robbers are going to say to themselves: "There's a law against my owning guns and, therefore, I should obey it,"

Jacob G. Hornberger, *Liberty*, June 1999.

One year after the mass confiscation of handguns, homicides in Australia have increased 3.2%. Assaults have risen by 8.6% and armed robberies have increased by a whopping 44%. In one state (Victoria), homicides with firearms have risen 300%, despite the government ban. The figures on armed robberies are especially instructive, since these crimes in particular had been falling for some 25 years. Now all of a sudden, with privately owned guns outlawed, they start increasing dramatically.

Similar statistics come from Great Britain, long the gun controllers' showcase country. There, where privately owned handguns were effectively banned a few years ago after a mass shooting by a crazed homosexual, crime figures show an increase in England and Wales for the first time in six years. The number of robberies, mostly mugging, increased by 19%. Violent offenses increased by 5%, and sexual offenses rose by 2%. Statistics from the Home Office show that the city of London suffered the greatest increase in crime—22%.

The United States

In the United States, however, violent crime continues to fall, for reasons no one seems to be able to figure out. The high rate of incarceration and the aging of the criminal population are often cited, but the increase in concealed carry laws, which let law-abiding citizens carry concealed firearms, is not often mentioned among the reasons for the drop in violent crimes in this country. University of Chicago economist John Lott is one expert who has shown there is a very real link between the decline of violent crime and the availability of firearms; his book, *More Guns, Less Crime*, has been virtually ignored by the establishment media.

But the connection ought to be obvious enough. When law-abiding people have guns and criminals know they have them, it's the criminals who have reason to be afraid, and they pick on softer targets that can't shoot back. When guns are criminalized, as in most crime-ridden American cities and in countries like Japan, Australia, and Great Britain, only the yakuza and its cousins around the world will have guns, and it's the law-abiding who have to live in fear.

"*Firearms are the single thread connecting every schoolhouse mass murder [that occurred between 1997 and 1999].*"

Gun Control Will Reduce School Violence

Cynthia Tucker

In the following viewpoint, Cynthia Tucker asserts that recent mass murders at schools have occurred because young people have too easy access to firearms. According to Tucker, adolescents have always been cruel to one another, but when angry teens have access to guns, they kill more people than they could with knives or other weapons. Tucker argues for more laws regulating firearms in order to reduce the likelihood of more school shootings.

As you read, consider the following questions:

1. According to Tucker, what weapons did Eric Harris and Dylan Klebold use unsuccessfully during the Columbine school shooting?
2. How many guns are in circulation in the United States, according to Tucker?
3. In the author's opinion, what gun regulations should be adopted in order to reduce school shootings?

L et's leave the "why" of the 1999 Columbine [school] massacre [in Littleton, Colorado] to the experts—the child psychologists, the family counselors, the ministers and rabbis—and wish them luck. A platoon of psychiatrists could study [the young gunmen] Eric Harris and Dylan Klebold for decades without finding a key to those hearts of darkness.

Let's turn instead to the "how" of it—something that anyone with common sense can easily discern. How? With guns, that's how. Understanding that obvious truth should keep us from feeling helpless, as if this madness is beyond our ability to change. It isn't.

There are factors in this strange episode that probably are beyond us. Adolescents will continue to be cruel to each other, no matter how much counseling or sensitivity-training they receive. Some parents will continue to delude themselves into believing their children are little angels when, instead, they are young sociopaths. And those young sociopaths will continue to dream up ways to wreak havoc in the lives of others. Such is the way of things.

Angry Young Men

But those angry young men cannot do it so well without guns. Without guns, Harris and Klebold would have had to settle for fewer than 13 victims. Their pipe bombs were not as deadly as they had hoped. A propane bomb they assembled to detonate in the school cafeteria did not go off. But their guns—exquisite tools for killing—got the job done.

Couldn't two angry thugs find other weapons if guns were not available? Of course they could. But none is as efficient as firearms. Baseball bats? Knives? There is a good reason you have never heard of a schoolhouse baseball-bat massacre. You can tackle a baseball-bat wielding sociopath. You might outrun a nut with a knife. But the victims at Columbine High School had no chance against two deranged young men armed with not only pipe bombs but also two sawed-off shotguns, a semiautomatic rifle and a semiautomatic pistol.

Firearms are the single thread connecting every schoolhouse mass murder of 1997 to 1999, from Pearl, Miss., to

Paducah, Ky., to Jonesboro, Ark., to Springfield, Ore., to Littleton, Colo. Other factors vary: The Jonesboro shooters, Mitchell Johnson, 13, and Andrew Golden, 11, were too young to have stored up grudges from years as social outcasts. The parents of the Springfield, Ore., shooter, 15-year-old Kip Kinkel, could hardly be suspected of inattention; they had their son in therapy.

Guns Are a Constant

But the guns are a constant—guns too easily available to kids who think killing is cute or clever. There are about 220 million guns in circulation in this country, which has a population of about 260 million people. The ratio is creeping toward one firearm for every man, woman and child.

Deep into Darkness

There have always been outcast kids, but today's outcasts can descend into [the video game] Doom or the World Wrestling Federation (WWF) or Marilyn Manson, they can commune with like-minded losers on Internet hate sites and not feel so alone. And once their rage is stoked and justified, once they're deep into the darkness and set to let loose as kids have long done in fast cars or on bad drugs or simply with a clothesline in a closet, they can grab a handy semiautomatic and, borrowing cool moves from the latest mayhem flick, go blow away their classmates.

Bob Levin, *Maclean's*, May 3, 1999.

The National Rifle Association (NRA) downsized its Denver convention and urged "prayer" for the Littleton victims. But it is still in the business of blocking even the most limited controls on firearms, which are easier to get your hands on than antibiotics for a sinus infection. Americans sickened by the constant spectacle of children dead at the hands of other children should stop allowing the NRA to carry the day.

It is not too much to expect that adults who own guns will be required to lock them away or face criminal penalties. It is entirely sensible to require firearms manufacturers to install mechanisms to prevent a gun from being fired by anyone other than the owner. (Gun manufacturers are exempt from the consumer safety laws that cover all other products, including toy guns.)

The NRA has the simplest of answers: Just lock up anyone who uses a gun to commit a criminal offense. I'm all for that. But that would not have deterred the homicidal-suicidal impulses of Harris and Klebold, would it?

"Additional gun-control laws will not necessarily prevent determined youths from obtaining firearms. More important, such laws will do nothing to address violence that is not gun related."

Gun Control Will Not Reduce School Violence

Timothy Brezina and James D. Wright

Timothy Brezina and James D. Wright argue in the following viewpoint that passing additional legal restrictions on youths' legal access to guns will fail to reduce school violence. They contend that most young people obtain firearms through illegal channels and would continue to do so no matter what new gun laws are passed. Brezina and Wright believe that addressing the factors that contribute to youth violence would be a more effective response to school shootings than increasing America's dependence on laws. Timothy Brezina is an assistant professor of sociology at Tulane University, and James D. Wright is the Charles and Leo Favrot Professor of Human Relations in the department of sociology at Tulane University.

As you read, consider the following questions:
1. What is the chance of dying a violent death at school, according to the authors?
2. As stated by Brezina and Wright, what are straw purchases?
3. In the authors' opinion, why are legal sanctions not effective deterrents?

Excerpted from "Going Armed in the School Zone," by Timothy Brezina and James D. Wright, *Forum for Applied Research and Public Policy*, Winter 2000. Copyright © 2000 by the University of Tennessee. Reprinted with permission.

On the morning of April 20, 1999, two students drove onto the Columbine High School campus in Littleton, Colorado, equipped with explosive devices, knives and guns, including two sawed-off shotguns, a rifle, and a semiautomatic handgun. In just 16 minutes, the gunmen fired more than 100 rounds, killing 13 and wounding 21 more before shooting themselves. The Littleton tragedy, the deadliest incident of school violence in U.S. history, aroused panic in the hearts of parents across the United States, and placed new pressure on legislators to pass stricter gun-control laws.

Political Reactions to School Shootings

A noteworthy reaction by lawmakers was that of California Assemblyman Dick Floyd, a Democrat who had until then remained silent on the issue of gun legislation. Prior to a vote placing new restrictions on handgun sales, he stated, "I am no longer going to be a nonparticipant. I am willing not only to vote for everything, I'll co-author every gun bill that comes along."

The issue, moreover, cut across party lines. In Colorado, Congressman Tom Tancredo, a Republican with libertarian leanings—recently elected with the aid of a sizable donation from the National Rifle Association—felt the pressure from his constituents. A resident of Littleton who lived just six blocks from Columbine High School, Tancredo told reporters that he could not simply go home and tell neighbors and friends that he had failed to act on the gun issue.

In fact, Tancredo was the only one of the six representatives from Colorado to vote for the House gun-control bill. Had the bill passed, it would have placed additional restrictions on semiautomatic rifles and high-capacity ammunition clips. Back in his home state, the congressman explained that the Columbine incident was a seminal event demanding unconventional action. "It will always be in our hearts as something that changed our lives," he said. "It made us do things we would not have done before."

Yet in a subsequent interview with reporters, Tancredo suggested that the steps Columbine made him take were not necessarily inspired by wisdom or forethought. Instead, he referred to gun control as a superficial response to deeply rooted social problems and admitted that the legislation he voted for in the House would have done nothing to stop the Columbine killings.

The heart of much recent debate over gun control is whether stricter laws would substantially alleviate the problem of school and youth violence. To answer that question, we must understand the ways that violent youths obtain access to guns, the scope of existing gun-control laws, and the likely impact of additional gun-control measures on the problem before us.

Perspective on Violence

Heightened media attention, especially to homicides with multiple victims, has led the public to believe that school violence is a growing problem. In fact, the total number of school-related violent incidents, including suicides and homicides, has steadily declined since the 1992–1993 school year, as have overall incidents of youth violence. The chance of dying a violent death at school is still less than one in a million.

Although the levels of serious school violence—including homicide, robbery, rape, sexual assault, and aggravated assault—remain unacceptably high, most serious violence occurs outside schools, on neighborhood streets or in the home. Students are three times more likely to be victims of a violent crime away from school than on school property, at a school-sponsored event, or on the way to or from school.

To be sure, the number of multiple-victim homicides has increased in recent years, but fortunately the incidence of such acts remains extremely rare. Since August 1995, an average of just five such acts has occurred each year. Considering the number of children that attend school in the United States—50 million or more—and the number of hours they spend in school each year, multiple-victim homicides at school are "the statistical equivalent of a needle in a haystack."

Because school-related violent deaths are rare and isolated, we must be very cautious about drawing conclusions or generalizations from them. Nevertheless, recent incidents raise many questions about kids and guns, specifically about the likely impact of popular gun-control proposals. The first question is how violent youths gain access to firearms.

Easy Access

How do kids get their hands on guns? This question is often posed as if there were some mystery about it. In fact, guns are easy to obtain. An estimated 200 million firearms are currently in circulation in the United States, and some 40 percent of all households own at least one gun.

In 1991, criminologists Joseph Sheley and James Wright interviewed more than 800 incarcerated juvenile offenders to gauge how hard it would be for them to get a gun when they were released from jail. Even though these juveniles couldn't legally purchase a gun because of their age and criminal record, 70 percent said they would have "no trouble at all" obtaining one. For inner-city high school students answering a similar question, 41 percent believed they could get a gun with no trouble at all; an additional 24 percent said getting a gun would be "only a little trouble." Adolescents in the general population, when asked about the availability of guns, provide somewhat smaller estimates, but the data confirm rather than challenge the fact that guns are not difficult for youths to obtain.

In the same study, juvenile inmates and high school students were asked how they would obtain guns. These respondents reported that family, friends, and street sources are the main sources of guns for juveniles. Evidently, perpetrators of school gun violence obtain guns in the same manner. In the school shooting sprees of the past decade, most of the perpetrators obtained guns from their own households or from the usual sources—parents and grandparents, occasionally from friends, and sometimes from street sources or theft. The shooters in Littleton obtained all of their guns illegally through straw purchases—that is, using older friends and acquaintances to buy the guns for them.

The Scope of the Law

For many people, it is shocking that guns are so easily accessible to youths. This state of affairs, however, is not the result of a large gap in the law. Moreover, the passage of additional legal restrictions will do little to rectify the situation, since most of the avenues through which youths obtain guns are already against the law.

Federal law already prohibits juveniles from purchasing guns through normal retail outlets. The legal age for purchasing firearms at such outlets is 18 for rifles and shotguns and 21 for handguns. Federal and state laws also prohibit persons of any age from carrying guns without a permit and bringing a gun onto school property. And most municipalities have local ordinances that ban the discharge of a firearm within city limits.

Gun Socialization

A July 1993 U.S. Department of Justice study found that "boys who own legal firearms . . . have much lower rates of delinquency and drug use [than those who obtained them illegally] and are even slightly less delinquent than nonowners of guns." It concluded "for legal gunowners, socialization appears to take place in the family: for illegal gunowners, it appears to take place on the street."

Stricter gun laws have served only to change the pattern of firearm access, fueling the black market. Forty years ago, kids could buy guns over the counter, and it was considered normal for them to carry and own guns for hunting and recreation. No Littleton-style shootings occurred in 1959, however.

Joanne Eisen and Paul Gallant, *Guns Magazine*, January 2000.

Although age restrictions are readily circumvented through the use of intermediaries and straw purchases, this too is illegal. Friends, acquaintances, and drug dealers who provide juveniles with firearms are at the least contributing to the delinquency of a minor and probably violating a dozen other laws as well. For example, Mark E. Manes—the 22-year-old man who provided the Columbine killers with a semiautomatic handgun—was charged with several felony counts: one for supplying a handgun to a minor and one for possession of a sawed-off shotgun. He was sentenced to six years in prison.

Nevertheless, the 1991 survey found that 32 percent of juvenile inmates and 18 percent of inner-city high school students had asked someone else to purchase a gun for them in a gun shop, pawnshop, or other retail outlet. And, as the Columbine shooters explained in a home-video tape, had it not been for Mark E. Manes they "would have found someone else."

So long as guns are available to anyone, they will also be available to any juvenile with the means and motive to exploit his network of family, friends, and acquaintances for the purpose of obtaining a firearm. However much we wish it to be otherwise, there is no plausible way to limit juvenile access to guns except to limit general access to guns, just as there is no plausible way to approach the problem of child poverty except by addressing the poverty of parents. There is, in turn, no practical way to limit general access to guns without doing something about the 200 million firearms already in circulation. It is by no means obvious how that could or should be accomplished. We are forced to ask, then, whether more or different laws will provide a solution.

Popular Proposals

After the Columbine incident, state and federal lawmakers proposed a variety of gun-control measures. Much of the attention focused on bills that would place further restrictions at the point of sale—measures such as extending background checks to all buyers at gun shows and extending the waiting period for background checks. Other bills would ban the manufacture or importation of certain additional types of firearms and high-capacity ammunition clips, require trigger locks or other safety devices on all guns sold, and create liability for gun owners who do not store their firearms in a safe and secure manner.

Given the ease of acquiring guns through intermediaries and straw purchases, the potential impact of further point-of-sale restrictions is not at all clear. Additional bans on specific types of guns and ammunition, moreover, would do nothing to curb access to guns already in circulation. For example, the manufacture of the combat-style TEC-9 semiautomatic handgun—one of the weapons used by the Columbine shooters—was outlawed in 1994, but that gun remains widely available.

Laws that encourage the safe and secure storage of firearms appear promising at first glance. Many gun owners keep and store firearms in irresponsible ways, a point that gun enthusiasts acknowledge and lament.

But safe-gun technologies—trigger locks and smart guns—are no panacea. The principal aim of safe-gun technologies is to reduce the incidence of accidental discharge of firearms. Yet most of the gun violence that befalls young people is intentional, not accidental. Fatal gun accidents have always been the least important component in the annual death toll. Thus, even if successful, safe-gun technologies will have little effect on the death toll from firearms.

There is a second and more fundamental reason safe-gun technologies are unlikely to have a substantial impact: "safe gun" is an oxymoron. The entire point of a firearm is that it be able to inflict grave harm and to do so reliably, efficiently, and decisively. The only real gun safety consists of well-trained, responsible users.

Ultimately, by passing more laws, and failing to understand the limits of the law, we may fool ourselves into believing that something important has been done about the problems of violence and youth. For example, legislators who promoted similar restrictions in the past, and who saw them become federal law under the Gun Control Act of 1968, believed they would "substantially alleviate" the problem of gun use by juvenile delinquents. . . .

Cops-and-Courts Fallacy

Gun-control opponents and advocates alike share great faith that the criminal justice system can prevent and deter crime through legal restrictions or crackdowns and punishment. The criminal justice system has an obvious and critical role to play. But as criminologist Marcus Felson warns, "It is easy to exaggerate the importance of the police, courts, and prisons as key actors in crime production or prevention."

First, most crimes do not come to the attention of officials, in part because victims fail to report them. Even when victims report a crime to the police, the prospect of apprehending a suspect is not very good. For example, less than half of all reported violent crimes end with an arrest, and the figure is much lower for property crimes. As the criminal justice funnel narrows, fewer cases are deemed suitable for prosecution, and fewer still lead to conviction and punishment. Thus official punishment, while it can be extreme, tends to be rare and uncertain. This, of course, is not the fault of criminal justice personnel. They are merely subject to the practical limits of law and law enforcement "in society as we know it."

[Moreover, most research indicates that legal sanctions are not particularly effective or meaningful deterrents, most likely because punishment is uncertain at best, and when it does happen, it is delayed. People are deterred from criminal involvement mainly because of informal and nonlegal sanctions such as the anticipation of a negative reaction from significant others, the expectation of guilt or shame for violating personal moral standards, and other stakes in conformity.

It is, therefore, not surprising that gun-control laws typically have little or no effect on rates of violent crime. At best, the effects are modest and short-term. According to the results of a recent evaluation published in the Journal of the American Medical Association, the 1994 Brady Law—which requires a background check and waiting period for the purchase of handguns from licensed dealers—is no exception.]

In short, uncritical faith in the criminal justice system is part of the problem. The cops-and-courts fallacy leads us to place unrealistic demands on the criminal justice system in hopes that some fine-tuning of the system here or there will produce dramatic effects on behavior. The cops-and-courts fallacy also contributes to severe dependence on the law and discourages the consideration of non-legal and possibly more-effective responses to crime. . . .

A Better Response

The gun-control response to school violence illustrates some of the problems that arise when social policy is driven by extreme and unusual cases. Additional gun-control laws will not necessarily prevent determined youths from obtaining firearms. More important, such laws will do nothing to address violence that is not gun related. Yet this type of violence—the bullying, harassment, fist fights, and knife wielding that can occur at any school—is much more typical and undoubtedly contributes to much of the gun-related violence that does occur.

A better response to school and youth violence is to address the problems that confront youths in their immediate environment, including obstacles to conventional success and the social strains and personal antagonisms that can provoke or escalate aggression. A number of prevention and early intervention programs have demonstrated positive long-term effects on behavior in rigorous evaluations and might serve as models for other communities. Such programs include "antibullying" campaigns, the implementation of anger-management, impulse-control, and problem-solving curricula at schools, and the provision of earlychildhood education and family support services for urban, low-income families.

It remains to be seen whether such programs can be replicated successfully on a wide scale, especially since many people believe that the problems of crime and violence can be solved by creating new laws and applying rougher penalties. When asked to identify the main source of blame for the crime problem, the majority of respondents in a 1994 national survey blamed the criminal justice system and, presumably, its lenient treatment of offenders. This exaggerated dependence on the law helps explain why so little effort has been spent getting to the root of the problem.

It also remains to be seen whether prevention and early intervention programs will receive adequate funding in the future. The number of dollars currently allocated to prison construction and get-tough measures far exceeds the number allocated to the type of programs described above. Regardless, it is difficult to see how more gun-control laws will alleviate the problem of youth violence, because such laws fail to address the immediate conditions of life that lead youths to carry guns and to break the law in the first place.

> "*The gun industry conducts itself without regard for public safety precisely because it bears none of the costs of that conduct.*"

Gun Manufacturers Should Be Held Responsible for Gun Violence

Dennis Henigan

In the following viewpoint, Dennis Henigan asserts that gun manufacturers have failed to take reasonable steps to make their products safer and to keep them out of the hands of criminals. According to Henigan, as a result of gun makers' irresponsibility, taxpayers pay billions of dollars a year in costs associated with gun violence. The author contends that only by holding gun manufacturers accountable in court will gun makers begin making guns safer and ensure that they are used responsibly. Henigan is director of the Center to Prevent Handgun Violence's Legal Action Project, which helps represent victims of gun violence in suing manufacturers.

As you read, consider the following questions:
1. What city became the first to sue gun makers, according to Henigan?
2. According to Henigan, what unsafe product was Ford Motor Company held liable for in court?
3. How much do direct and indirect costs of gun violence amount to per year, as reported by the author?

On Oct. 30, 1998, New Orleans became the first city to sue gun makers. Mayor Marc Morial, with the assistance of the Legal Action Project of the Center to Prevent Handgun Violence, has filed a lawsuit against the industry for designing and marketing handguns that lack basic safety features which would prevent shootings by children, teenagers and other unauthorized users. New Orleans seeks to hold the industry accountable for the cost of police, emergency and health-care services that the city pays for due to gun injuries and deaths that would be prevented if gun manufacturers were more responsible in the design of their products.

Since Oct. 30, four other cities—Chicago; Miami-Dade County, Fla.; Bridgeport, Conn.; and Atlanta—have filed lawsuits, and more are sure to follow. While some of these lawsuits follow New Orleans', citing the industry's inexcusable failure to make its products safer, others—particularly Chicago's—focus on the industry's negligent distribution and marketing practices that contribute to a massive illegal gun market.

Although the gun industry claims these lawsuits have no legal merit, it seeks to prevent the courts from deciding the matter. Its longtime front group, the National Rifle Association, or NRA, is pushing for special legislative protection to ensure that judges and juries never hear these cases. A bill which creates immunity from liability exclusively for the gun industry has been enacted in Georgia. A Florida bill would make the mayor of Miami-Dade County a felon for continuing his lawsuit. Other state legislatures are considering similar bills.

Not content to stop there, Georgia Republican Rep. Bob Barr, a board member of the NRA, has introduced a bill that would limit lawsuits against the industry by local governments and private citizens. Like the state bills, Barr's bill is a patent attempt to intimidate mayors and others who seek to hold the gun industry accountable for its unnecessarily dangerous products and irresponsible marketing practices.

Legal Precedents

What possibly could justify legislative action to block these lawsuits? The gun lobby's arguments reveal a remarkable ignorance of basic principles of American tort law. First, the lobby's spokespeople have argued that gun manufacturers cannot be liable unless their products don't work. According to this argument, only the gun owner whose gun doesn't shoot straight can sue a gun manufacturer. This simply is not true. According to long-accepted principles of product-liability law, a product can be defective in design regardless of whether it malfunctions.

The Ford Motor Co., for example, was liable for fires caused by the placement of its Pinto fuel tank. Even though the fuel tank did not cause the car to malfunction, the placement of the tank created an unreasonable risk that passengers would be incinerated following a collision. Similarly, the failure of gun manufacturers to install safety devices to prevent gun accidents makes guns unreasonably dangerous even if they reliably shoot bullets.

Second, the industry also claims that it cannot be liable because its products are legal. This argument confuses criminal liability, which applies only to illegal conduct, with civil liability, which does not. Most of civil tort law concerns the liability of parties whose actions, though they may be legal, nevertheless are irresponsible and expose others to unreasonable risk of harm. Ford's placement of the Pinto gas tank did not violate any statute, but it created a significant hazard for which Ford was liable.

Moreover, people (and companies) whose conduct violated no law can be held liable for increasing the risk that someone else will act illegally. In 1997, the Florida Supreme Court ruled unanimously that Kmart was liable for selling a rifle to an intoxicated buyer who then shot his girlfriend. Kmart's sale of the gun violated no statute but was so irresponsible that the company was held answerable for the harm caused. Saying that an industry's practices violated no statutes is no defense.

Third, the gun industry also confidently asserts that it cannot be liable when its products are misused by others. If we adhered to this principle generally, we never would have held auto manufacturers liable for selling cars without seat belts and other safety features because most car accidents are caused by driver error.

Reducing Risk

The law wisely imposes a duty on manufacturers to do what they can to reduce the risk of foreseeable injury, even when the wrongful conduct of another is a more direct cause of the harm. Recently, the Ohio Supreme Court held that the maker of a disposable lighter may be liable for failing to use feasible means to protect against misuse by children. The court wrote: "[A] product may be found defective in design . . . where the manufacturer fails to incorporate feasible safety features to prevent harm caused by foreseeable human error." That is precisely the basis for the New Orleans lawsuit: Because the gun industry is well aware that many gun owners make the mistake of leaving guns accessible to children who then misuse them, it should be liable for its failure to use feasible safety systems to prevent this foreseeable, and tragic, misuse of its products. And, as Kmart learned, gun sellers can be liable even when the misuse is criminal.

Avoiding Responsibility

Robert Hass, former senior vice president for marketing and sales for Smith & Wesson . . . asserts that "the company and the industry as a whole are fully aware of the extent of the criminal misuse of handguns. . . . In spite of their knowledge, however, the industry's position has consistently been to take no independent action to insure responsible distribution practices."

David C. Anderson, *American Prospect*, September/October 1999.

Holding companies liable for increasing the risk of injury from misuse does not shift the blame away from other culpable parties. It makes all parties who contributed to the harm responsible for their conduct. The law should punish the reckless driver but not immunize the automaker who could have made the car safer. The law should punish the criminal who uses the gun, but it should not immunize an industry if it fails to take reasonable steps to ensure that criminals cannot misuse the gun. And we are not talking simply about the criminal use of guns. The gun industry is shockingly indifferent to the suicides and unintentional shootings that could be averted if they included basic safety features which would prevent children from using them. When the industry markets guns with so little trigger resistance that a 2-year-old can fire them, why should the blame rest only on the toddler and on the parents who made the gun accessible? Gun manufacturers have the capability to prevent these tragedies from happening. Why should they escape all accountability for failing to do so?

Disingenuous Arguments

The gun lobby insists that these lawsuits are an improper use of the courts to resolve issues that should be decided by state legislatures. If we want to change the way guns are designed and sold, this argument goes, then such changes should be made by legislatures, not courts. If this argument justifies blocking lawsuits against the gun industry, then it would apply to other industries as well. Yet, the courts did not dismiss the liability lawsuits against Ford on the grounds that the only remedy for victims of exploding Pintos was to seek greater safety regulation of autos from Congress.

This argument is simply disingenuous. The gun industry hardly would support greater regulation imposed by Congress. The industry always has resisted any kind of reform.

One purpose of product-liability law is to encourage manufacturers to increase product safety. This is particularly compelling in the case of firearms. Guns, unlike any other consumer product, are exempt from regulation by the Consumer Product Safety Commission. Having used its lobbying clout to protect itself from safety standards, the gun industry now seeks to shield itself from accountability to those injured by its conduct.

The industry's argument of last resort is that the lawsuits are nothing more than greedy lawyers seeking to extort legal fees by threatening a legitimate industry. This argument mimics the response of every industry under legal attack for selling unreasonably dangerous products. It essentially amounts to a strategy of changing the subject. Finding it difficult to defend its conduct, the gun industry makes an issue of the lawyers attacking it.

Of course, the lawyers for the cities will receive contingency fees (a percentage of any award) only if these lawsuits are successful. In contrast, the defense lawyers for the gun industry, who are paid hundreds of dollars per hour, will be paid regardless of whether the industry is vindicated.

A Small Industry Inflicts Huge Costs

The gun industry is a relatively small one that inflicts huge costs on society. Annual sales estimates run anywhere from $1.7 billion to $9 billion. Meanwhile, direct and indirect costs of gun violence amount to more than $23 billion a year, most of which is borne by taxpayers. Given that much of these costs are the result of shootings the industry could prevent, the industry's irresponsibility effectively is being subsidized by taxpayers. Why should this subsidy be allowed to continue?

The gun industry conducts itself without regard for public safety precisely because it bears none of the costs of that conduct. Although it would be entirely fair to shift those costs, the primary purpose of these lawsuits is not to recover damages but to change the way the industry does business.

The mayors who already have filed lawsuits and those who are considering filing are not going to be intimidated by the legislation proposed by Barr. It is not these lawsuits which are frivolous, but his legislation, which grants exclusive immunity to gun manufacturers and denies these mayors and private citizens the fundamental right to be heard in a court of law.

The gun industry has a choice: It can continue business as usual, but only if it pays its fair share of the cost, or it can take the necessary and feasible steps to reduce the misuse of its products by children and criminals. For creating this dilemma for the gun industry, the mayors should be praised, not condemned.

"*The ultimate result, if the lawsuits against gun manufacturers are successful, would be to reduce the access to firearms by citizens, thus making the public less safe.*"

Gun Manufacturers Should Not Be Held Responsible for Gun Violence

H. Sterling Burnett

H. Sterling Burnett is a senior policy analyst for the National Center for Policy Analysis, a non-partisan, non-profit research institute. In the following viewpoint, Burnett maintains that holding gun makers responsible for gun violence is bad law because it allows the courts to legislate gun policy when such laws should be enacted by publicly-elected legislators. Burnett also contends that lawsuits against gun makers would make society less safe by restricting the legal availability of firearms, which are used more often to stop crimes than to commit them. Moreover, the author claims that the lawsuits would have the most adverse effect on the poor and minorities, who live in the most crime-ridden areas and depend upon guns for self-defense.

As you read, consider the following questions:
1. According to criminologist Gary Kleck, how many times are guns used defensively per year?
2. What percentage of persons defending themselves with guns during an assault are injured, as reported by Burnett?
3. According to the author, what percentage of all murder victims are minorities?

Following their successes in forcing tobacco companies to cough up billions of dollars to the states, trial lawyers have convinced several big-city mayors to sue gun manufacturers to recover the costs of gun violence in their cities.

Subsequently the mayors of New Orleans, Chicago, Atlanta, Miami-Dade County, Cleveland, St. Louis, Los Angeles, San Francisco, Cincinnati, and Bridgeport, Conn., started the trend by filing lawsuits against gun manufacturers to allegedly recover costs related to firearm violence in their cities. And even more municipalities seem likely to file suit in the near future. They say they're looking for reimbursement for the public health and safety costs associated with treating and preventing injuries caused by firearms used in crimes.

Two types of suits are moving through the courts based upon two different (but equally dubious) sets of arguments. One group of lawsuits purports that guns are a public nuisance and gun manufacturers knowingly flood cities with more guns than they could expect to sell to law-abiding citizens, thus arming criminals (Chicago was first to assert this). The second group of suits charges that guns, as they are currently manufactured, are unreasonably dangerous because gun makers have allegedly failed to implement safety devices that would prevent unauthorized users from firing guns (New Orleans initiated this claim).

If these city officials succeed, these lawsuits will establish bad law and bad public policy—even outside the firearms industry.

Gun Lawsuits Are Bad

This trend is establishing bad law because the suits ask the courts to legislate. As much as some may wish it, the U.S. does not have a *pure* free-market economy with respect to consumer goods. As part of the political process, legislatures often control, limit or prohibit access to some products, such as tobacco, guns and prescription drugs. It's a delicate balancing act to give a free people access to certain products while maximizing public safety.

These lawsuits against gun makers would replace the will of the majority (as expressed through the legislature) with the determinations of an unelected judiciary. Lawsuit proponents, unable to convince legislators that removing guns from the hands of law-abiding citizens will reduce crime, are trying to use the courts to impose their views on a skeptical public.

Support for Lawsuits

Do you support or oppose governments suing gun manufacturers for the cost of violent crime?

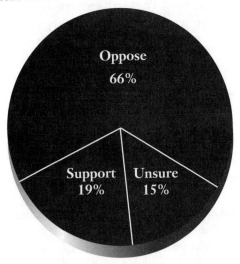

DecisionQuest, *Wall Street Journal*, 1999.

And thus far, the courts have resisted the urge to legislate gun policy. In more than 40 similar lawsuits brought typically by crime victims, courts have consistently decided that questions about whether firearms should be legal and widely available are for legislative assemblies to decide. For instance, in the 1996 case of *Wasylow v. Glock, Inc.*, the court ruled that "It is the province of legislative or authorized administrative bodies, and not the judicial branch, to advance through democratic channels policies that would directly or indirectly either 1) ban some classes of handguns or 2) transform firearm enterprises into insurers against misuse of their products. Frustration at the failure of legislatures to enact laws sufficient to curb handgun injuries is not adequate reason to engage the judicial forum in efforts to implement a broad policy change."

In addition, holding the gun makers responsible for criminal misuse of their products, as these suits would do, would also reverse a sound and well-established principle in product-liability law: Manufacturers of any type are not responsible for the criminal or negligent misuse of their non-defective products. And the guns in question are not faulty in any way.

If gun makers are to blame when their products are misused, what products are safe? Knives, cars and many household products are used each year to commit crimes. And accidents involving automobiles, ladders, swimming pools and private airplanes cost the public millions of dollars annually. Should the manufacturers of these products compensate the public for the costs incurred when people drown, or when they die in automobile accidents or falls? If this is the new product-liability standard, then we will have to forego the benefits of these products. Some companies, unable to survive the lawsuits that would be filed, would go out of business; others might simply move overseas to countries that still hold individuals, rather than inanimate objects, responsible when they act in a criminal, stupid or negligent manner.

Bad Public Policy

Even if these lawsuits were not dubious as a matter of law, they would still be open to criticism as harmful public policy. Why? Because of a fundamental point that the mayors and other anti-gun interests conveniently overlook: *Guns actually prevent more crimes than they cause, and in fact they save society money.* I recently completed a study for the National Center for Policy Analysis that indicates the savings.

Guns are used for self-defense somewhere between 800,000 and 3.6 million times per year (in the vast majority of cases, merely showing the firearm prevents the crime). A comprehensive study conducted by Gary Kleck, a criminologist from Florida State University, estimated defensive gun uses at more than 2.5 million per year. This far exceeds the number of crimes committed with firearms in 1996:

- 483,000 according to the Bureau of Justice Statistics; or

- 915,000 if you look at the National Crime Victimization Surveys.

Using estimates for the cost of firearm violence from several different studies, I calculated the benefits from defensive gun use each year. Using the firearm crime and defensive gun use figures most favorable to advocates for stricter gun control, I found that the benefits from defensive gun use exceed the costs of violent firearm crimes (the costs the mayors want the gun manufacturers to pay for) by between $90 million and $3.5 billion. Using the most credible estimate for defensive gun uses, the benefits range from $1 billion to $38 billion.

Putting these dollar figures in more human terms: *Guns save lives.* The fact is that the best defense against violence is an armed response. For example, women faced with assault are 2.5 times less likely to suffer serious injury if they defend themselves with a gun rather than responding with other weapons or by offering no resistance. Additionally, persons defending themselves with guns during an assault are injured only 12 percent of the time, compared to 25 percent for those using other weapons, 27 percent for those offering no resistance and nearly 26 percent for those who flee. It becomes obvious that firearms are the safest, most effective way to protect oneself against criminal activity—which is why American police officers carry guns rather than going unarmed or merely carrying knives.

The ultimate result, if the lawsuits against gun manufacturers are successful, would be to reduce the access to firearms by citizens, thus making the public less safe. It is unlikely that the gun industry would cease to produce and sell firearms, even if it were to lose this legal battle. Instead, it is likely that the price of firearms would increase substantially to cover increased liability insurance coverage and to pay for expanded sales-monitoring programs and personalized gun safety technologies. Another possible outcome is that smaller gun manufacturers or those with slim profit margins would go bankrupt while more successful firms would survive, but shift from the civilian gun market and focus their efforts on providing firearms to the police and military. Obviously, this would also drive up the cost of firearms to civilians and cops.

Relatively affluent Americans would still be able to afford to purchase guns for self-defense and sport, while the urban poor (typically minorities), who already suffer the most from criminal depredation, would be placed at even greater risk due to their reduced financial ability to purchase firearms. This is particularly unfortunate when you consider that persons in poor households experience nearly twice as much violent crime as persons at every other income level. In fact, inner-city residents are approximately 33 percent more likely to suffer a violent crime than suburban residents, and 40 percent more likely than rural residents.

Studies also show that minorities, who make up a disproportionate share of the population of large urban areas, are three times more likely to be robbed, twice as likely to suffer aggravated assault, and make up half of all murder victims although they represent only 12.6 percent of the population.

Thus, higher gun prices would disarm precisely those individuals who are most likely to face violent crime and who would benefit most from easier access to guns and more widespread gun ownership.

If gun makers are either bankrupted or forced to cease (or nearly cease) civilian production, the black market in firearms would only become larger as the value of guns would increase due to the dearth of new guns entering the market.

Federal law currently allows private citizens to sell some or all of their guns without regulation as long as it is not a regular business enterprise. . . . As gun values rise, private sales of firearms would likely increase, with some people amassing entire arsenals "off the books." In addition, the higher prices that guns would fetch on the black market would make gun thefts more profitable and thus more likely.

Since retail firearms sales to private citizens currently subsidize the cost of guns to local police, federal agents and the military, the price of guns to law enforcement and military personnel would also increase in the absence of the civilian market.

Legislative Reaction to the Lawsuits

For these reasons, the lawsuits are backfiring in several state legislatures and in Congress where it seems that banning gun lawsuits, not guns, is an idea whose time has come. Georgia was one of the first states to enact legislation forbidding cities from suing the gun industry.

Then going a slightly different direction, Wyoming lawmakers have introduced a bill encouraging the state's attorney general to intervene on behalf of gun manufacturers in liability lawsuits.

On a federal level, Rep. Bob Barr (R-Ga.) has introduced legislation in the U.S. House of Representatives that would ban frivolous lawsuits against the gun industry (H.R. 1032, the Firearms Heritage Protection Act).[1] Conversely, an Illinois congressman introduced a bill the very next day to accomplish just the opposite.

Lawsuits Harm Cities, Not Help Them

The lawsuits against the gun industry will not reduce crime, poverty, homelessness, improve the schools, or fill potholes. Guns are not the cause of our cities' ills; they are just scapegoats for the mayors' inability to significantly curb crime.

If the suits result in a decline in lawful gun ownership, crime and unemployment would likely increase as citizens are left defenseless against criminal violence and industries flee to friendlier and safer business environments.

Mayors and trial lawyers may disagree with this assessment of the merits of this legislation, but then they rarely live in the areas where crime is most rampant and police response times are slowest. And, of course, they will be raking in the cash if gun makers buckle in to the extortion these lawsuits pose—money can blind even the best-intentioned people from the needs of those less fortunate.

Tobacco vs. Gun Lawsuits

Though much has been made of the comparison between the gun lawsuits and the recently settled tobacco lawsuits, there is much to distinguish guns from cigarettes. Guns do not cause harm to the user nor to third parties when used responsibly.

That guns are potentially dangerous is widely known and has never been disputed by the firearms industry. However

---

1. H.R. 1032 is currently being reviewed by the House Committee on the Judiciary.

unlike tobacco, guns produce a multitude of tangible social goods: pleasures obtained by those involved in the shooting sports, U.S. national security, police-led crime prevention and criminal apprehension efforts, as well as effective personal defense against crime.

Only a small fraction of firearms, far less than 1 percent, are ever involved in violence. The clearest evidence indicating that even the mayors suing the gun industry believe guns are beneficial is the fact that they arm their police. It is not that guns are bad; it is that some people use them badly.

The rationale is no more valid to sue gun manufacturers for the improper use of their products than there is to sue knife manufacturers (or the makers of various blunt objects) which are used in violent crimes, all of which can result in costs to governments.

When filing their lawsuits, each of the mayors cited the substantial burden which gun-related violence imposes on the public coffers in their cities. It is clear that the cost of gun violence is substantial and, unlike the fiscal benefits provided by defensive gun use, it is relatively easy to measure or quantify. It is difficult, however, to account for both the number of crimes prevented and the savings to society from crimes *not* committed or thwarted by defensive gun use. However difficult to quantify, my research shows that those benefits far exceed the cost of gun violence. More crimes are prevented by guns in the hands of law-abiding citizens every year than are committed with guns—and the savings to cities from these defensive gun uses (and the general savings to society from gun ownership) dwarfs the cost of gun violence to municipalities.

| *"Safer guns would seem to be in the long-term interest of those who support the right of honest citizens to own firearms."*

Gun Safety Standards Should Be Mandatory

Gregg Easterbrook

In the following viewpoint, Gregg Easterbrook claims that gun safety devices such as trigger locks would greatly reduce the incidence of gun deaths. He argues that mandatory gun safety standards would not violate citizens' constitutional right to own firearms because the Second Amendment gives power to the states to regulate guns. According to Easterbrook, mandatory gun safety standards would merely regulate guns in the same way that other consumer products are regulated in an effort to improve public safety. Gregg Easterbrook is a senior editor for the *New Republic* and Beliefnet.com.

As you read, consider the following questions:

1. According to Easterbrook, how many Americans died in firearm accidents in 1996?
2. How much do magazine safety devices cost, as stated by the author?
3. According to the author, what percentage of Americans favor gun-safety regulation?

Two of the four weapons used in the 1999 Columbine High massacre [in Littleton, Colorado, which resulted in fifteen dead], the Hi-Point 9mm carbine and the Intratec TEC-DC9 semiauto, are popular on the gun circuit because they look zoomy. The Intratec is designed to look like something used by commandos, the Hi-Point to look like a weapon issued to space marines for combat in orbit. The popularity of these guns reminds us that weapons manufacturers constantly redesign their products for appearance, features, and targetmarket appeal. Don't want futuristic, for instance? Then check out Smith & Wesson's "Ladysmith" gun series, designed with that feminine touch. Design features added to guns for marketing purposes are often as cosmetic as the features of car or clothing marketing—the TEC-DC9 may give users a commando feel, but no genuine commando would ever wield this inaccurate and jam-prone hunk of junk. Of course, that does not prevent them from being deadly to the helpless.

But, though gun manufacturers invest considerable sums in designing for appearance and firepower, what they don't design for is safety. As a gun owner, I think it's time they did.

Safety and Guns

"Safety" and "gun" are not mutually exclusive terms. Something that does intentional harm should also be engineered not to do unintended harm. Yet, while the design of firearms has been extensively elaborated in recent decades for such harmful characteristics as rate of fire, the safety engineering of guns has scarcely changed since the time of [American manufacturer of firearms] Samuel Colt. In 1996, the most recent year for which statistics are available, 1,134 Americans died in firearm accidents, 135 of the dead being children. Most of these fatalities were caused by the lack of safety engineering. Just try to imagine any other product still being marketed unchanged if inherent design faults caused a thousand accidental deaths annually. Why shouldn't the same logic that has been used to require recent gains in the safety of cars also be applied to guns?

People who don't own a gun may not appreciate how ridiculous most firearms are from the standpoint of safety engineering. Only a small percentage of guns, for instance, have internal safeties that prevent them from firing if dropped. Internal safeties are cheap and reliable: one of the deadliest new weapons on the market, the Austrian-made Glock pistol, has this feature, which could easily be added to all guns. The manual safeties on the outside of most guns are often poorly labeled, confusing to operate, or hard to see—the safety on my Savage 69RXL twelve-gauge shotgun has its designations imprinted so deep into the metal you practically need a flashlight to tell whether it's on or not. (The weapon's owner's manual actually says, under a section titled "ten commandments of firearms," "1. Don't rely on your gun's safety.") There's no requirement that guns even have manual safeties, and some do not.

Horsey. © 1999 by *Seattle Post Intelligencer.* Reprinted with permission of North America Syndicate.

Also unchanged since the nineteenth century is the fact that it often requires labored inspection to determine whether a gun is loaded. For revolvers, you must look closely along the axis of the barrel, which is not exactly the world's greatest idea if the gun is loaded. For most shotguns and for pistols whose magazines snap into the grip, there is no way to tell from appearances whether the weapon is ready to fire.

And, for most guns, it is nigh unto impossible to know whether a round is chambered. That fact is deceptively dangerous. Popular firearms such as the AR15 rifle or the Beretta 9mm handgun seem harmless if the clip has been removed, but a bullet may sit unnoticed in the chamber. Perhaps a quarter of annual gun-death accidents occur when people fail to realize a round is chambered in an "empty" gun. This mistake is amazingly easy to make: I'm a college graduate, and that didn't stop me from once accidentally discharging a handgun after snapping out the clip but forgetting to check the chamber. (Fortune smiled and I only killed a couch.)

The simple addition of a magazine safety prevents chambered-round accidents. But the majority of gun manufacturers haven't incorporated this device, though Smith & Wesson has begun embossing a cheerful warning disclaimer about chambered rounds on some pistols. Magazine safeties cost less than $2 each. Every gun for sale in the United States could have this feature for a total cost that for new guns works out to roughly $30,000 per life saved in chambered-round accidents—making the magazine safety extremely attractive from the standpoint of the eternal benefit-cost tradeoff.

Improvements in Gun Safety

There has been some halting action in the direction of improved gun safety. A few manufacturers now include trigger locks with each gun sale; after Columbine, President Clinton proposed national legislation requiring trigger locks. Trigger locks would not have prevented Columbine High, but they might save hundreds of lives per year without one whit of firearm-freedom loss. Several handgun companies are experimenting with a fire-confirmation system that in theory would render pistols inoperative for anyone but their owners. (When shooting, owners would wear a ring that broadcasts a security code to the gun; the hitch is that kids or thieves might take the ring when taking the gun.) The Hi-Point carbine was conceived to appeal to gun fanciers, but at least its designer took the precaution of engineering the weapon so that it cannot physically accommodate the assault-style magazines that have no legitimate sporting or self-defense purpose. These are steps in the right direction.

But it's time to rethink gun engineering from the ground up, bringing firearms out of the antebellum era and into the technological age from the standpoint of the systems-engineering approach that has made so many other products safer. Trigger locks, for example, should not be add-ons that the buyer can simply discard. My cheap, reliable cell phone won't work unless I punch a four-digit code; why isn't my gun the same? (In an emergency, I'd rather fumble to punch a code than fumble to load.) Every gun should be designed so that it's completely obvious whether the weapon is loaded—transparent magazines, say. Safeties should be standardized and color-coded for rapid reading. Some visible cue should make it obvious whether a gun has a chambered round. (In addition to reducing gun accidents, making it visually obvious whether a firearm is loaded or chambered would be a boon to police.) Internal and magazine safeties should be ubiquitous. Firing actions should be redesigned so that it's not physically possible to convert semiautomatic weapons into illegal full automatics. Ammunition systems should be redesigned so that they cannot be converted for assault-style clips designed to spray death in all directions.

Safe Gun Engineering Is Not Gun Control

Safe gun engineering has nothing to do with gun control. Today, government requires extensively detailed safety engineering for many products that are dangerous but only lightly controlled, such as automobiles, and for products that are completely uncontrolled, such as toys, furnaces, and baby strollers. It's preposterous to think that as a society America imposes rigorous safety-design standards on strollers but merrily exempts firearms from the benefits of modern safety engineering, allowing gun manufacturers to continue using design assumptions that date to Colt's tinker's shop.

Ideally, gun manufacturers would offer safer designs of their own accord. But marketing experience has shown that, although police departments, hunters, and sport shooters will buy gun-safety features, significant elements of the gun market probably won't—gun buyers who are criminals, for example, have as a class not shown themselves to be overly concerned with public safety. In pure textbook theory, we'd let gun buyers sort out their own safety choices and pay for the level of risk they accept. But gun buyers aren't making safety decisions solely for themselves; they impose their choices on the people they might accidentally shoot. Thus, public safety dictates a gun-safety regulatory standard.

Needless to say, the gun lobby will fight firearm redesign, but does National Rifle Association (NRA) opposition have any meaning to anyone anymore, other than to the sold-out? For responsible political leaders, or responsible firearm owners, to contend they can't advocate safer guns because the gun nuts will howl is an indictment of the responsible, not of the nuts. Gun proponents constantly say they oppose controls but favor safety. Let's call them on this claim and demand a national initiative to reinvent the gun with safety in mind.

Is Safety Constitutional?

Would the right-to-bear-arms clause of the Constitution permit this idea? Because the preamble of the Second Amendment places gun ownership in the context of the raising of state militias—an anachronistic goal the NRA today methodically fudges—the Supreme Court has given states broad discretion in gun statutes. This means there is little doubt states could legislate firearm safety standards. Congress probably has the power to do so, too, though legal challenges are inevitable. The Second Amendment specifies a right to bear arms but also that firearms be "well-regulated," and, in this context, the Supreme Court has upheld national restrictions against the sawed-off shotgun and automatic weapons. Gun-safety engineering wouldn't stop individuals from owning weapons—it would require only that their weapons incorporate the best available safety features.

And, as an added bonus, if there were firearm-safety standards, many of the manufacturers stung by new design engineering costs would be foreign. As Tom Diaz points out in his new book, *Making a Killing: The Business of Guns in America*, a surprising percentage of the companies flooding U.S. gun shows and Kmarts with firearms are foreign-owned—Beretta being an Italian firm, Browning being Japanese-owned, Smith & Wesson being English, Germany's Heckler & Koch and Austria's Glock being leading U.S. gun suppliers, and the Chinese (who generally bar their own citizens from owning guns) selling in the United States about half the rifles imported here. When European politicians prattle on in high dudgeon about the shocking American gun culture, they never pause to add that it is their own corporations busily exploiting and encouraging that culture; roughly half the guns sold in the United States are imported, mainly from Europe, with the firearm import sector growing much faster than domestic manufacture. It might be argued that European and Asian firms are dumping unsafe guns here—not only mass-marketing the types of weapons favored by criminals (such as North China Industries' SKS assault rifle, which is similar to the AK-47) but also shipping, by the millions, firearms that lack basic safety features. If the United States were exporting cars without seat belts to Italy, Germany, or China, those nations would be apoplectic. Why is it OK for their companies to ship to us firearms without magazine safeties?

Liability Suits

It's possible that, if gun manufacturers begin to lose liability suits, they will adopt safety engineering for reasons of legal exposure. Generally, liability law allows products to be dangerous if they are obviously dangerous, in the way that cigarette lighters obviously cause open flame. Absurdly, gun makers' legal departments may fear that adding safety features will increase liability by reducing the obviousness of danger. But such problems as the lack of magazine safeties create firearm dangers that aren't obvious, more akin to the Pinto gas tank [which exploded in rear-end collisions] than the Bic lighter; considerations such as these may eventually lead to plaintiffs' victories in liability suits against gun manufacturers. Why endure another decade of avoidable gun-accident deaths as the lawsuits mount rather than working for safe-gun engineering right now?

Safer guns would seem to be in the long-term interest of those who support the right of honest citizens to own firearms for hunting, self-defense, and sport shooting. And public support appears evident: polls show that 68 percent of Americans favor gun-safety regulation. But if Congress lacks the will or courage to take on the NRA, there is another way the national government could assume the lead.

Firearms aficionados pine for guns with the latest military features: folding stocks, banana clips, laser sights, black-carbon finish, flash suppressors, and so on. Suppose the Pentagon reengineered its guns with safety in mind. Defense Department contractors have both the technical know-how to accomplish breakthroughs in firearm design and the financial incentive that flows from the dollar volume of Pentagon purchasing. If the Defense Department made a commitment to safer guns, training accidents would decline, the technology of gun safety would be advanced—and safety might become cool and high-tech rather than square, because everything the military does with guns is copied by the gun culture. Something to think about.

> *"Mandating locking guns or locking guns up suggests we have a problem because some guns aren't locked up. . . . The real problem lies in a lack of education and proper supervision."*

Gun Safety Standards Should Not Be Mandatory

Phil W. Johnston

Phil W. Johnston asserts in the following viewpoint that gun owners who live in a free society should voluntarily take steps to lessen the risks associated with private gun ownership instead of being forced to do so by the government. He contends that safety features such as trigger locks can make guns less effective for self-defense purposes and endanger the lives of gun owners. Moreover, Johnston argues that guns are not as dangerous as many people think they are—for example, more children drown in pools than die in firearms accidents. Phil W. Johnston writes for *Gun News Digest*.

As you read, consider the following questions:

1. According to Johnston, how many people died in snowmobile accidents in Minnesota in 1997?
2. How many Americans lost their lives in firearms accidents in 1993, as reported by the author?
3. According to Johnston, how many children died in firearms accidents in 1993?

There are several ways to start this piece. I could start it with a 5-year-old child wandering into the master bedroom while his/her mom is talking on the phone and dad is away at work, for instance. There's a loaded .357 magnum in the bedside stand—you see how this is going to develop. Then there's the other possible scenario—you're fast asleep when you hear the window shatter—you quickly grab that same .357 and use it to instantly stop a felon who is bent on your personal destruction. If the gun had been locked up—maybe there wouldn't have been time.

Owning a firearm is not a decision to be taken lightly. In the right hands, of course, we all realize that a firearm is nothing more or less than a tool—one capable of being routinely used for entertainment, winning medals, hunting or defending the home. On the other hand, when a firearm falls into the wrong hands it can become a weapon, instantly turning a mindless individual into a creep who uses the arm to terrorize our society.

The third possible situation comes into play when a child, children, or even an impaired adult gets mixed up with a firearm. We've all seen or heard the stories, although amazingly rare in such a large society as ours.

Freedom Has a Price

When I begin thinking of the philosophical basis for firearms ownership, the first thought that pops into my head are the words of Harlon Carter [the late National Rifle Association Executive Vice President] when he told NRA members that "freedom has always had a price. . . ." When a huge free society owns millions of arms, there will always be a few tragic individual cases prompted by gunowners who "forgot the rules of safety, for just an instant" or of Americans who lose their life to criminals who should have never been on the street in the first place. It's like living with the costs of flying, or just traveling. Traveling has its risks, regardless of the mode of transportation. We accept the risk and live with the odd tragic loss of human life. Even when we know that tens of thousands of Americans die or are maimed for life by drunken or otherwise impaired drivers, we simply shake our heads and go on—accepting the risk—the cost if you will.

In . . . Minnesota 32 people have been killed just on snow-mobiles in 1997. We're evidently perfectly willing to accept this tragic risk, and cost, it seems, too. These are all costs associated with a free society.

We're becoming a society that seems to think that we can legislate solutions to problems that, a generation ago, would have never cropped up. Today, we ask our legislators, educators, or possibly even our church to take care of our problems at home. They're our problems—not their problems. Firearms ownership is a logical place to begin this debate.

Population Shift

Over the past century the population of the United States has shifted from a rural setting to one which now places most Americans in an urban lifestyle which resembles little else, it seems. Once we consisted of a society that often used a firearm to routinely put food on the table and almost as often relied on a firearm for entertainment as well. It was common to find a loaded .22 rifle for instance, leaning in the corner, ready to dispatch the skunk or raccoon that raided the garden, or pot a rabbit for dinner. A generation ago, we grew up with guns. . . . In rural North Dakota, guns were and still pretty much are, a way of life. My dad taught me how to handle a gun when I was old enough to wonder about such things and he left a lasting impression on me when he used a Winchester Model 12, 12 gauge shotgun to blast open an old upright freezer at the dump with a load of buckshot. I'll see that destructive power until I die. The point was of course, that a firearm deserved respect. I don't ever remember dad locking anything up as I grew up. Nor do I remember mom locking up chemicals that were routinely used for cleaning chores back then either.

When Cindy and I raised our kids, we routinely had firearms coming out of our ears it seemed. I was shooting hand-gun competition each weekend and both our children would follow in my footsteps. Guns have been a way of life for us and no gun was off limits to our youngsters. We told both of them to ask first and we showed both of them how to check and unload every gun that they'd ever see. We taught them both that they never point the muzzle at anything or anyone they didn't want to harm and we taught them that the only "safety" was the person holding the gun. Both kids grew up with firearms and they knew how to handle them safely by the time they could walk. When they were old enough, we taught them how to drive, safely, we hope.

Today, it seems, we've lost sight of taking care of our own lives. Now we're asking others to take care of our problems. Today, making the choice to legally own a firearm, for whatever reason, is becoming far more difficult, and even dangerous in some situations, it seems.

Ramirez. © 2000 by *Los Angeles Times*. Reprinted by permission of Copley Media Services.

Recently, President Bill Clinton suggested that handgun owners should own and use trigger locks or some other device to secure a firearm, and we've seen legislation in 15 states which imposes various penalties on parents or guardians who let minors get their hands on a gun and then subsequently hurt someone with that gun. Often this legislation suggests that the person could be successfully charged, and I presume convicted, when he or she "should reasonably have known" that a minor could get their hands on a gun in the home.

Off the bat, this doesn't look like too bad an idea. It makes sense to keep 'em locked up and out of harm's way, doesn't it? It looks like a good idea until you get back to the basic reason that one might keep a firearm in the first place. If we keep a defensive gun locked up in one place with the ammunition locked up in another place as is often suggested in "10 Commandment" types of safety suggestions, we'd be hard pressed to get the gun, load it, and present it IN TIME to make a difference. Millions of times each year in the United States, firearms are used by law abiding citizens to save lives. That fact isn't often reported by our media, of course.

Impose Penalties

While most US legislation is thus far aimed at imposing penalties on adults who permit a minor under the age of 14 to get a gun and then harm someone with it, often the law suggests that one is guilty of a crime if one knew or "should have known" that a kid could reach a gun in the house and the gun wasn't secured in some manner. In Maryland for instance, ". . . an individual may not store or leave a loaded firearm in any location where the individual knew or should have known that an unsupervised minor would gain access to the firearm." Minnesota "Imposes a gross misdemeanor penalty on any person who negligently stores or leaves a loaded firearm in a location where the person knows or reasonably should know a child under age 14 is likely to gain access, unless reasonable action is taken to secure the firearm against access by the child." Such wording makes it clear that indeed, gun ownership has taken on new meaning.

Our most rabid anti-gun legislators are now suggesting that handguns, at least, be marketed complete with some type of trigger locking device in the future. I suspect that these same legislators will, in their infinite wisdom, subsequently suggest that Americans will soon thereafter be somehow negligent if we fail to use these locking devices, *all the time*.

When one decides to own a firearm, obviously there are some things to keep in mind, whether the gun is locked up or not. A gun is not safe just because it is secure. The only safe gun is a gun that is in good hands. Having a loaded firearm in the home shares common ground with keeping a large sharp knife in the kitchen. Both require education and common sense.

Equating the ownership of firearms with other dangers encountered in life or costs of living is indeed justified. While some argue that our politicians and anti-gun zealots are simply looking out for us when they legislate against the gun owning public, that doesn't seem to be the case.

Relative Risks

According to the most recent vital statistics available, in 1993,1,521 Americans lost their lives to firearms accidents while 16,381 more used firearms to take their own lives (66% of the total suicides). To make gun locking devices a mandatory or even a strongly suggested measure seems to be an answer for the proverbial non-problem. A trigger lock surely won't prevent a suicidal person from unlocking the device and then pulling the trigger. If on the other hand we're looking to save the lives of our children, we would gain far more ground if we could keep our kids away from water (1,247 accidental drownings), drugs and medicines (590 accidental poisonings) or fire (1,063 children died from burns)! Of course the leading danger to our kids takes place when we put them in our car and hit the highways and byways of the United States. We killed 5,503 of our kids in cars in 1993! I didn't mention firearms accidents because they're at the bottom of the accidental death list—392 kids lost their lives to firearms accidents. Nearly 200 of our kids died because of falls!

Like purchasing a firearm, the decision to lock or not remains a personal decision. . . .

US and Canadian gunowners to be sure would be wise to keep their eyes on pending legislation on their local levels as well as the national scene. Mandating locking guns or locking guns up suggests that we have a problem because some guns aren't locked up (nor will they be). The real problem lies in a lack of education and proper supervision—all the time. We don't need a Government entity suggesting that we do either.

Periodical Bibliography

The following articles have been selected to supplement the diverse views presented in this chapter. Addresses are provided for periodicals not indexed in the *Readers' Guide to Periodical Literature*, the *Alternative Press Index*, the *Social Sciences Index*, or the *Index to Legal Periodicals and Books*.

Angie Cannon	"The New Smart Guns," *U.S. News & World Report*, January 24, 2000.
James K. Hahn	"Use Law to Force Changes," *Los Angeles Times*, May 31, 1999.
Jacob G. Hornberger	"Gun Control Would Make Us Less Safe," *Liberty*, June 1999.
Gary Kleck	"Guns Aren't Ready to Be Smart," *New York Times*, March 11, 2000.
David B. Kopel	"Taking It to the Streets: Treating Guns Like Cars," *Reason*, November 1999.
John R. Lott Jr.	"Gun Licensing and Registration Leads to Increased Crime, Lost Lives," *Los Angeles Times*, August 23, 2000.
John R. Lott Jr.	"Gun Show: Why Gun Laws Will Not Prevent Public Shootings," *National Review*, May 31, 1999.
New Republic	"Yelling 'Fire!'" April 3, 2000.
Newsweek	"Guns in America: What Must Be Done," August 23, 1999.
Jeremy Rabkin	"Beware the Attack Lawyers," *American Spectator*, June 1999.
Bruce Shapiro	"The Guns of Littleton," *Nation*, May 17, 1999.
Susan B. Sorenson	"Regulating Firearms as a Consumer Product," *Science*, November 19, 1999.
Michael W. Warfel	"Why Gun Control? An Individual's Right to Own and Bear Arms Must Be Balanced by the Greater Social Needs of a Society," *America*, April 15, 2000.
Woody West	"Gun Control Still Is Not Thug Control," *Insight on the News*, January 24, 2000.

For Further Discussion

Chapter 1

1. The Violence Policy Center contends that an increase in gun buying consistently leads to an increase in homicide and suicide rates. However, Don B. Kates Jr. argues that although gun buying and crime rates have gone up at the same time, this correlation does not prove that an increase in gun ownership *causes* the increase in violent crimes. On the contrary, he claims that an increase in crimes such as homicide often results in an increase in gun buying for self-defense. In your opinion, which author is more convincing? Cite specifics from each viewpoint to construct your answer.

2. Hillel Goldstein describes being shot to help support his argument that private gun ownership can protect people from mass murderers such as Adolf Hitler. Conversely, Roger Rosenblatt quotes prominent people such as historians to support his argument that depending on privately owned guns to guarantee liberty can lead to anarchy. In your opinion, which author uses evidence more convincingly? In general, do you think personal anecdotes or appeals to authority are more convincing? Please explain.

3. Miguel A. Faria Jr. contends that doctors exaggerate the public health risk of gun violence in order to obtain research grants from the federal government. However, Richard F. Corlin argues that increasing rates of gun violence constitute a serious health hazard. Does the fact that Corlin is a physician strengthen or weaken his argument? That is, do you think most Americans trust doctors to provide them with objective and accurate information on public health risks? Or do you think Americans are wary of doctors? Please explain your answer.

Chapter 2

1. Dave LaCourse argues that the Supreme Court decision *U.S. v. Miller* made it clear that the Second Amendment grants individuals the unrestricted right to own firearms. However, Robert Simmons contends that the *Miller* decision recognized an individual's constitutional right to own firearms only if his or her intent was to participate in a militia. Examine how both authors use the *Miller* decision to bolster their arguments. In your opinion, which author uses the case more convincingly? Why?

2. Joseph Sobran claims that the Second Amendment—which he argues grants individuals the unrestricted right to own firearms—was intended as a bulwark against tyranny. On the other hand, Charles L. Blek Jr. contends that the right to own guns should be restricted in the same way that other rights are curtailed in order to lower rates of gun violence. In your opinion, is the threat of government tyranny or the prevalence of gun violence a more serious concern today? Please explain your answer.

Chapter 3

1. John R. Lott Jr. argues that guns are an effective means of self-defense. However, David Johnston contends that few people actually use guns as a means of self-defense because they are unable to arm themselves quickly enough. Examine the evidence that each author uses to support his argument and decide which is more convincing. Please explain your answer.

2. Frank J. Murray contends that guns are used often by individuals to defend themselves from criminals. On the other hand, Tom Diaz claims that gun manufacturers and gun magazines exaggerate the extent to which guns are used defensively in order to sell their products. Examine the evidence that both authors provide and determine which author you find most convincing. Be as specific as possible when explaining your answer.

3. One of the issues central to the debate about whether to allow citizens to carry concealed weapons is the question of whether such ready access to firearms would lead to an increase in impulse killing. In your opinion, how likely is it that an altercation between two people would result in an impulse shooting if one or both individuals were carrying a concealed weapon? Please cite the viewpoints of Morgan Reynolds and H. Sterling Burnett and Handgun Control, Inc. when explaining your answer.

Chapter 4

1. Dennis Henigan maintains that gun manufacturers should be held responsible in court for costs associated with violent crime. On the other hand, H. Sterling Burnett claims that gun laws should not be decided in court. In your opinion, should gun makers be held responsible for the actions of those who purchase their products? Include in your answer a discussion of personal versus corporate responsibility.

2. Gregg Easterbrook argues that gun manufacturers should be required to make firearms that meet minimum safety standards. However, Phil W. Johnston contends that safety should be the responsibility not of gun manufacturers but of individual gun owners. Do you think safety devices such as trigger locks, seat belts, and helmets should be required by law in order to improve public safety? Why or why not?

Organizations to Contact

The editors have compiled the following list of organizations concerned with the issues debated in this book. The descriptions are derived from materials provided by the organizations. All have publications or information available for interested readers. The list was compiled on the date of publication of the present volume; information provided here may change. Be aware that many organizations take several weeks or longer to respond to inquiries, so allow as much time as possible.

American Civil Liberties Union (ACLU)
132 W. 43rd St., New York, NY 10036
(212) 944-9800 • fax: (212) 869-9065
website: www.aclu.org

The ACLU champions the rights set forth in the Declaration of Independence and the U.S. Constitution. It opposes the suppression of individual rights. The ACLU interprets the Second Amendment as a guarantee for states to form militias, not as a guarantee of the individual right to own and bear firearms. Consequently, the organization believes that gun control is constitutional and that because guns are dangerous, gun control is necessary. The ACLU publishes the semiannual *Civil Liberties* in addition to policy statements and reports.

Cato Institute
1000 Massachusetts Ave. NW, Washington, DC 20001
(202) 842-0200 • fax (202) 842-3490
website: www.cato.org

The Cato Institute is a libertarian public-policy research foundation. It evaluates government policies and offers reform proposals and commentary on its website. Its publications include the Cato Policy Analysis series of reports, which have covered topics such as "Fighting Back: Crime, Self-Defense, and the Right to Carry a Handgun," and "Trust the People: The Case Against Gun Control." It also publishes the magazine *Regulation*, the *Cato Policy Report*, and books such as *The Samurai, The Mountie, and The Cowboy: Should America Adopt the Gun Controls of Other Democracies?*

Center to Prevent Handgun Violence
1250 I St. NW, Suite 802, Washington, DC 20005
(202) 289-7319
websites: www.cphv.org • www.gunlawsuits.com

The center is the legal action, research, and education affiliate of Handgun Control, Inc. The center's Legal Action Project provides free legal representation for victims in lawsuits against reckless gun manufacturers, dealers, and owners. The center's Straight Talk About Risks (STAR) program is a violence prevention program designed to help youth develop victim prevention skills and to rehearse behaviors needed to manage conflicts without violence or guns. Its websites provide fact sheets and updates on pending gun lawsuits.

Citizens Committee for the Right to Keep and Bear Arms
12500 NE Tenth Pl., Bellevue, WA 98005
(206) 454-4911 • fax: (206) 451-3959
website: www.ccrkba.org

The committee believes that the U.S. Constitution's Second Amendment guarantees and protects the right of individual Americans to own guns. It works to educate the public concerning this right and to lobby legislators to prevent the passage of gun control laws. The committee is affiliated with the Second Amendment Foundation and has more than six hundred thousand members. It publishes the books *Gun Laws of America*, *Gun Rights Fact Book*, *Origin of the Second Amendment*, and *Point Blank: Guns and Violence in America*.

Coalition for Gun Control
PO Box 395, Station D, Toronto, Ontario, Canada M6P 1H9
fax: (416) 604-0209
www.guncontrol.org

The coalition was formed to reduce gun death, injury, and crime. It supports the registration of all guns and works for tougher restrictions on handguns. The organization promotes safe storage requirements for all firearms and educates to counter the romance of guns. Various fact sheets and other education materials on gun control are available on its website.

Coalition to Stop Gun Violence
1000 16th St. NW, Suite 603, Washington, DC 20036-5705
(202) 530-0340 • fax: (202) 530-0331
website: www.csgv.org

The coalition lobbies at the local, state, and federal levels to ban the sale of handguns and assault weapons to individuals and to institute licensing and registration of all firearms. It also litigates cases against firearms makers. Its publications include various informational sheets on gun violence and the *Annual Citizens' Con-*

ference to Stop Gun Violence Briefing Book, a compendium of gun control fact sheets, arguments, and resources.

Doctors for Responsible Gun Ownership
The Claremont Institute
250 West First St., Suite 330, Claremont, CA 91711
(909) 621-6825 • fax: (909) 626-8724
website: www.claremont.org

The organization is comprised of health professionals familiar with guns and medical research. It works to correct poor medical scholarship about the dangers of guns and to educate people on the importance of guns for self-defense. The organization has legally challenged laws that regulate guns. Its publications include the booklet *Firearms: A Handbook for Health Officials*.

Handgun Control, Inc.
1225 I St. NW, Suite 1100, Washington, DC 20005
(202) 898-0792 • fax: (202) 371-9615

A citizens' lobby working for the federal regulation of the manufacture, sale, and civilian possession of handguns and automatic weapons, the organization successfully promoted the passage of the Brady Bill, which mandates a five-day waiting period for the purchase of handguns. The lobby publishes the quarterly newsletter *Progress Report* and the book *Guns Don't Die—People Do*, as well as legislative reports and pamphlets.

Independence Institute
14142 Denver West Pkwy., Suite 101, Golden, CO 80401
(303) 279-6536 • fax: (303) 279-4176
website: www.i2i.org

The Independence Institute is a pro–free market think tank that supports gun ownership as a civil liberty and a constitutional right. Its publications include books and booklets opposing gun control, such as "Children and Guns: Sensible Solutions," "'Shall Issue': The New Wave of Concealed Handgun Permit Laws," and "Unfair and Unconstitutional: The New Federal Gun Control and Juvenile Crime Proposals," as well as the book *Guns: Who Should Have Them?* Its website also contains articles, fact sheets, and commentary from a variety of sources.

Jews for the Preservation of Firearms Ownership (JPFO)
PO Box 270143, Hartford, WI 53207
(262) 673-9745 • fax: (262) 673-9746

JPFO is an educational organization that believes Jewish law mandates self-defense. Its primary goal is the elimination of the idea that gun control is a socially useful public policy in any country. JPFO publishes the quarterly *Firearms Sentinel*, the booklet "Will 'Gun Control' Make You Safer?" and regular news alerts.

Join Together
441 Stuart St., Boston, MA 02116
(617) 437-1500 • fax: (617) 437-9394
e-mail: info@jointogether.org • website: www.jointogether.org
Join Together, a project of the Boston University School of Public Health, is an organization that serves as a national resource for communities working to reduce substance abuse and gun violence. Its publications include a quarterly newsletter.

The Lawyer's Second Amendment Society
1077 W. Morton Ave., Suite C, Porterville, CA 93257-1989
e-mail: cyrano@ix.netcom.com • website: www.thelsas.org
The society is a nationwide network of attorneys and others who are interested in preserving the right to keep and bear arms. It attempts to educate citizens about what it believes is their inalienable right, provided by the Constitution's framers, to defend themselves with firearms, if necessary. The society publishes the *Liberty Poll* newsletter six times a year.

Million Mom March Foundation
San Francisco General Hospital, San Francisco, CA 94110
(800) RINGING
e-mail: national@millionmommarch.org
website: www.millionmommarch.org
The foundation is a grassroots organization that supports common sense gun laws. The foundation organized the Million Mom March, in which thousands marched through Washington, D.C., on Mother's Day, May 14, 2000, in support of licensing and registration and other firearms regulations. The foundation's website provides fact sheets on gun violence and gun control initiatives.

National Crime Prevention Council (NCPC)
1700 K St. NW, 2nd Floor, Washington, DC 20006-3827
(202) 466-6272 • fax: (202) 296-1356
website: www.ncpc.org
The NCPC is a branch of the U.S. Department of Justice. Through its programs and education materials, the council works to teach Americans how to reduce crime and to address its causes.

It provides readers with information on gun control and gun violence. NCPC's publications include the newsletter *Catalyst*, which is published ten times a year, and the book *Reducing Gun Violence: What Communities Can Do*.

National Rifle Association of America (NRA)

11250 Waples Mill Rd., Fairfax, VA 22030
(703) 267-1000 • fax: (703) 267-3989
website: www.nra.org

With nearly 3 million members, the NRA is America's largest organization of gun owners. It is also the primary lobbying group for those who oppose gun control laws. The NRA believes that such laws violate the U.S. Constitution and do nothing to reduce crime. In addition to its monthly magazines *America's 1st Freedom, American Rifleman, American Hunter, Insights,* and *Shooting Sports USA*, the NRA publishes numerous books, bibliographies, reports, and pamphlets on gun ownership, gun safety, and gun control.

Second Amendment Foundation

12500 NE Tenth Pl., Bellevue, WA 98005
(206) 454-7012 • fax: (206) 451-3959
website: www.saf.org

The foundation is dedicated to informing Americans about their Second Amendment right to keep and bear firearms. It believes that gun control laws violate this right. The foundation publishes numerous books, including *The Amazing Vanishing Second Amendment, The Best Defense: True Stories of Intended Victims Who Defended Themselves with a Firearm,* and *CCW: Carrying Concealed Weapons*. The complete text of the book *How to Defend Your Gun Rights* is available on its website.

U.S. Department of Justice

Office of Justice Programs
PO Box 6000, Rockville, MD 20850
(800) 732-3277
websites: http://ojjdp.ncjrs.org/gun/index.html
www.ojp.usdoj.gov/bjs/welcome.html

The Department of Justice protects citizens by maintaining effective law enforcement, crime prevention, crime detection, and prosecution and rehabilitation of offenders. Through its Office of Justice Programs, the department operates the National Institute of Justice, the Office of Juvenile Justice and Delinquency Prevention, and the Bureau of Justice Statistics. Its publications include fact sheets, research packets, bibliographies, and the semiannual journal *Juvenile Justice*.

Violence Policy Center
2000 P St. NW, Suite 200, Washington, DC 20036
(202) 822-8200 • fax: (202) 822-8202
website: www.vpc.org

The center is an educational foundation that conducts research on firearms violence. It works to educate the public concerning the dangers of guns and supports gun control measures. The center's publications include the report *Handgun Licensing and Registration: What It Can and Cannot Do*, *GUNLAND USA: A State-by-State Ranking of Gun Shows, Gun Retailers, Machine Guns, and Gun Manufacturers*, and *Guns for Felons: How the NRA Works to Rearm Criminals*.

Bibliography of Books

Jack Anderson   *Inside the NRA: Armed and Dangerous: An Exposé.*
                       New York: Dove, 1996.

Michael A. Bellesiles *Arming America: The Origins of a National Gun
                       Culture.* New York: Alfred A. Knopf, 2000.

John M. Bruce and   *The Changing Politics of Gun Control.* Lanham,
Clyde Wilcox   MD: Rowman & Littlefield, 1998.

Philip J. Cook and   *Gun Violence: The Real Costs.* New York: Oxford
Jens Ludwig   University Press, 2000.

Vic Cox   *Guns, Violence, and Teens.* Springfield, NJ:
                       Enslow, 1997.

Clayton Cramer   *Concealed Weapons Laws of the Early Republic:
                       Dueling, Southern Violence, and Moral Reform.*
                       Westport, CT: Praeger, 1999.

Jennifer Croft   *Everything You Need to Know About Guns in the
                       Home.* New York: Rosen, 2000.

Tom Diaz   *Making a Killing: The Business of Guns in
                       America.* New York: New Press, 1999.

Jan E. Dizard, Robert *Guns in America: A Reader.* New York: New
Merril Muth, and   York University Press, 1999.
Stephen P. Andrews Jr.,
eds.

Wilbur Edel   *Gun Control: Threat to Liberty or Defense Against
                       Anarchy?* Westport, CT: Praeger, 1995.

George A. Gellert   *Confronting Violence: Answers to Questions About
                       the Epidemic Destroying America's Homes and
                       Communities.* Boulder, CO: Westview Press,
                       1997.

James Gilligan   *Violence: Our Deadly Epidemic and Its Causes.*
                       New York: G.P. Putnam, 1996.

Jacob G. Hornberger   *The Tyranny of Gun Control.* Fairfax, VA: Future
and Richard M.   of Freedom Foundation, 1998.
Ebeling, eds.

Don B. Kates Jr. and   *The Great American Gun Debate: Essays on
Gary Kleck   Firearms and Violence.* San Francisco: Pacific
                       Research Institute for Public Policy, 1997.

Gary Kleck   *Targeting Guns: Firearms and Their Control.* New
                       York: de Gruyter, 1997.

Wayne R. LaPierre   *Guns, Crime, and Freedom.* New York: Harper-
                       Perennial, 1995.

John R. Lott Jr.	*More Guns, Less Crime: Understanding Crime and Gun-Control Laws*. Chicago: University of Chicago Press, 1998.
Maryann Miller	*Working Together Against Gun Violence*. New York: Rosen, 1997.
James M. Murray	*Fifty Things You Can Do About Guns*. San Francisco: Robert D. Reed, 1994.
Ted Schwarz	*Kids and Guns: The History, the Present, the Dangers, and the Remedies*. New York: Franklin Watts, 1999.
Joseph F. Sheley	*In the Line of Fire: Youth, Guns, and Violence in Urban America*. New York: de Gruyter, 1995.
Peter Squires	*Gun Culture or Gun Control: Firearms, Violence, and Society*. New York: Routledge, 2000.
Josh Sugarmann	*Every Handgun Is Aimed at You: The Case for Banning Handguns*. New York: New Press, 2001.
Glenn Utter	*Encyclopedia of Gun Control*. New York: Oryx Press, 1999.
William Weir	*A Well-Regulated Militia: The Battle over Gun Control*. North Haven, CT: Archon, 1997.

Index